From Barry Docks to
Las Palmas, harbour f
with an admiration son

What was not said abou~~~~ ~~~~ *Fidelity* until she
disappeared without trace one New Year's Eve?

Survivors from the ship, we have told the true story of
HMS Fidelity, and her strange skipper, to Marcel
Jullian.

In the hope that God will recognize his own.

    Lt.-Cmdr. PAT O'LEARY, GC, DSO, RN
    Lt. GEORGE ARCHIBALD, RN

Marcel Jullian

HMS Fidelity

Futura Publications Limited

A Futura Book

First published in Great Britain in 1957
by Souvenir Press Limited

First Futura Publications edition 1975

Told to MARCEL JULLIAN by
Lt.-Cmdr. PAT O'LEARY, GC, DSO, RN and
Lt. GEORGE ARCHIBALD, RN

First published in France as *HMS FIDELITY* by
Amiot-Dumont, Le Livre Contemporain, Paris

Translated by MERVYN SAVILL

ISBN 0 8600 72126

Printed in Great Britain by
Cox & Wyman Ltd,
London, Reading and Fakenham

Futura Publications Limited
49 Poland Street, London W1A 2LG

CONTENTS

List of the French and English Names of the Officers and Ratings of HMS Fidelity Mentioned in the Text

French Names	English Names	Nicknames
Costa	Langlais	
Passementton	Doudet	Uncle
Madeleine Guesclin	Barclay	Clébard
		(a mongrel bitch)
Soigne	O'Leary	Mortiss
Bernard	Archibald	Archie
Brinchant	O'Neill	Pipite
Grillo	Fontenay	
Lebasque	Lalande	
Marcelac	J. J. Avencourt	
Patte	Rogers	
Rinto	Lagrange	
Leblond	Richardson	
Ploëno		The Monster

The English names are all correct. The French names, however, including that of the ship, have been voluntarily changed. In this way we have conformed to the express order which Commander Langlais gave to his crew: 'In future you have only one name – your *nom de guerre*. You will no longer need your own, because I am leading you to your death.'

They obeyed. They fought, got married, were decorated and vanished under their *noms de guerre*.

CHAPTER ONE

OVERTURE TO DANGER

The first time Soigne saw *Le Rhône*, she seemed to him like a dream ship. Outlined against the Gibraltar sky, the cargo boat's hull was low in the blue water.

Soigne had come from the stoke-hole; his eyes, mouth and nostrils were full of coal. There are many varieties of coal in the world, but none could possibly have been as greasy as that carried by the infernal old British tub he had just left. The blackness stuck to his skin, closed the pores and prevented him from sweating. Its dust seeped everywhere; he blew it from his nose; he spat it out and it got into his eyes.

Soigne and his twelve companions were silent in the rowing boat which bore them towards *Le Rhône*. Had it not been for their Belgian officers' uniforms, they would have been taken for miners who had escaped from a fire-damp explosion. They had left their country and their army after the collapse of May 1940 and had experienced all the vicissitudes of the exodus. Weeks later, they had met again on the quayside at Sète in search of a ship whose captain would agree to take them out of France. All the captains refused. Finally the master of a collier took them aboard together with a large contingent of Czech troops. Herded between decks, their drinking water rationed, half stifled, they had crawled along the Spanish coast as far as Gibraltar, the collier's destination. The Admiralty having given no permission to come alongside, the vessel stagnated in the June heat, rocked by the choppy swell in the Bay, her rusty plates broiling in the sun.

They could have waited for many days had it not been for an

almost miraculous intervention. A French captain happened to be on board. He noticed a sailor with a red pompon on his cap rowing in the roadstead. He hailed him.

'Does there happen to be one of our ships in port?'

'Yes, *mon capitaine, Le Rhône.*'

'I don't care how you arrange it, *mon vieux,* but see that her captain gets me out of here.'

That afternoon, a pinnace flying the captain's flag, with a sailor in the bows, drew alongside the collier. Admiral Muselier had come in person to take delivery of one of the first naval paymasters who had rallied to the Free French.

On the following day the *Le Rhône* launch arrived to take off the Belgian officers.

The clearer the outline of the rescuing cargo ship grew, the more Soigne was convinced that it was a pleasure ship. It was painted in light colours, the tricolour fluttered proudly at the masthead and the well-polished brass gleamed in the sun. Brinchant, a small man with a rather childish face, standing next to Soigne, examined the vessel with a more impartial eye. She appeared to him greyish and old, bristling with derricks like a pin cushion, her rails faintly outlined with white.

However contradictory the impressions of the two men were, they tallied in one respect; the *Le Rhône* could not be an ordinary ship. The captain was standing at the top of the gangway; dressed in white from head to foot, a pipe between his teeth, he looked like an old sea dog in shoregoing rig.

Soigne thought he must be seeing things when, not far from the captain, he noticed a fair-haired girl in shorts and a white shirt. She was ensconced in a wicker chair, which she balanced on its back legs, her ankles resting on the rail. Her arms and legs were bare, and she observed the new arrivals without a trace of embarrassment.

Soigne caught hold of the manrope and began to climb up the gangway. At the top he thought that he would be welcomed by the captain, but a small sunburnt lieutenant with wide-awake eyes came towards him.

'I'm Lieutenant Costa, welcome to my ship.'

By the way he said 'my ship' anyone would have thought that it was his personal property.

Chewing on his pipe, the captain remained in the background. He evinced no surprise at his subordinate's behaviour. As soon as the last Belgian came aboard, Costa introduced the captain: 'Commandant Passementton,' and calmly gave the order to the old sailor: 'Uncle, look after these gentlemen.'

Soigne looked around for the female passenger. She had disappeared. The wicker chair now stood abandoned on the deck.

A sailor led the guests to the showers where they got busy removing the coal from their bodies. They had to scrub themselves almost raw to get a trickle of blackish water and to find below it the original colour of their skins. By dint of standing under the hot shower and rubbing themselves vigorously, the men looked like scalded pigs. After shaving and obtaining what clothes they could from the ship's shops, they tried to sum up the situation.

The attitude of the crew seemed strange. From time to time in the gangways they met small excited groups of sailors who fell silent at their approach. On the foc'sle, a hexagonal platform carried two twin ack-ack guns, an unusual feature in a merchant ship. When Soigne, taking the wrong door, went down into an open hold, he found it full of bicycles, barrels and various utensils which had been stowed in obvious haste. Brinchant, for his part, wondered what roles were played by the strange lieutenant who gave orders to the captain and the fair-haired girl who had been tanning her limbs in the midday sun ...

When the whole team came on deck about six o'clock that evening the waters of the roadstead were glittering. The shadow of the Rock began to engulf the lower houses and to outline on the hillside the black barrier, denoting the forbidden zone. Sensing the approach of night, the gulls skimmed restlessly over the waves. The heat was intense and the advertisements for English beer, visible in the distance on the yellow houses, only aggravated their thirst. 'Guinness is good for you' one of them read. Elsewhere were posters advertising cigarettes: 'Bandmaster', 'Timbalier' and a Spanish tyres poster obviously out of date and half torn. British soldiers in steel helmets were on guard between the blocks and the *Le Rhône*, on the quayside piled high with war material. With land well in view the Belgians, whom the port authorities had kept under observation for several days in their collier, felt rehabilitated. Costa addressed them:

'Gentlemen,' he said, 'if you will join me in the mess room we'll have a drink. And then we'll have a meal.'

The mess room was panelled in light wood with a horseshoe-shaped table. A bench ran along the bulkhead and on the inside of the horseshoe was a line of swivel chairs. The table was laid – white cloth, glasses, bottles of aperitif, fresh from the ice box. As soon as they were all present, Costa motioned them to be silent and, pointing to the woman passenger at his side, said:

'Gentlemen, may I present Mlle Madeleine Guesclin who does us the honour of living aboard.'

The lieutenant presided, with the captain on his left and the young woman on his right. Madeleine Guesclin had not batted an eyelid when all the men's eyes were turned on her. She was obviously used to living among men and her behaviour was free and easy. She was not pretty but her face, and in particular her eyes, could not fail to arouse interest. Two officers completed the ships staff.

The sun continued to sink over the roadstead. While the glasses were being filled, it turned the portholes to flame. A little copper plaque was screwed into the panelling behind the captain's head. A sunbeam fell on it and made it gleam lightly.

This plaque caught the visitors' eyes; it bore merely a date and a name: *10th May 1940 – Las Palmas.*

What could the *Le Rhône* have been doing six weeks ago in the Canaries?

'Gentlemen,' said Costa raising his glass, 'you must not imagine it was in the name of Franco-Belgian fraternity alone that I have welcomed you in my ship. Actually, I need you. The *Le Rhône* has been in port since the 20th June, and since that date I have been going day after day on board the ships which come alongside in search of volunteers. I am at Gibraltar today in order to play my part in this war. You, on the other hand, have just arrived from Belgium from which the Boches have thrown you out; we should get along well together.'

There was great power in his fruity southern voice as he stressed the words: 'To Belgium, gentlemen, to France!'

The toast was drunk and immediately afterwards conversation became general. 'I need you,' Costa had said. The Belgians wondered what was expected of them. Soigne, seated next to Marais, the chief engineer, pointed to the copper plaque. 'What does that represent?' he asked.

'Oh that?' replied the other. 'You'd better ask Costa.'

Costa again. It seemed as though the lieutenant was in complete command. At the moment he was talking and gesticulating wildly. On his left 'Uncle' was drinking his *pastis* with the air of a hardened drinker. Soigne turned to Brinchant and whispered in his ear. 'What do you make of it?'

'We've only got to be patient,' was the reply. 'We'll soon know a bit more.'

The dinner began. Very much at his ease, the lieutenant joined in all the conversations, repeatedly asking his new guests for details of their escape. The food was excellent but very highly seasoned.

Costa saw to it that there was no lack of wine.

'Blaise, you're leaving us to die of thirst.'

The steward continued to bring in new bottles.

13

'We have a hold full of vintage wine,' explained the lieutenant during the meal. 'That's right, isn't it, Uncle?'

The party was soon flushed with drink. A cheroot in the corner of his mouth, Captain Passementton guffawed at his table companion's story. Everyone spoke at the top of his voice; there was laughter and a clatter of plates.

Madeleine Guesclin alone was silent. Her thoughts seemed to be elsewhere. A stranger might have thought that she was irritated by this male conversation, where everyone was trying to shine. But there was something more than irritation in her behaviour. Soigne was the first to notice her anxiety and, from that moment, he did not take his eyes off her. The girl kept looking towards the door as though expecting someone. The Belgian caught her eye and was very much struck with the determination he saw in it. What was happening outside?

The storm suddenly broke without anyone knowing the precise reason. Costa raised his hand to claim attention and at his first words they all realized that things were serious.

'Gentlemen,' he said, 'I am ashamed to admit this to foreign officers, but I am in command of a phantom ship. Yes, I have just been betrayed by the majority of my crew. I thought I was dealing with sailors, but I was mistaken. Do you see that plaque? It recalls an exploit we carried out together. That was yesterday. This evening I have nothing left but a hotchpotch of milksops and cowards – good-for-nothings who do not even get a gutsache from the sufferings of their country. Kid glove sailors, chocolate box soldiers whom I ought to have strangled with my bare hands.'

His anger made him lean across the table; he spat out the words as though he were throwing stones. The sound of his own voice seemed to stimulate his excitement.

'But I haven't finished with those bastards. I know there are still some of them aboard torn between the fear that I shall smash their teeth in or that they will join their mates in the Gibraltar gaol. And they're supposed to be Frenchmen, gentlemen. Frenchmen? That rabble! I'll tell you how you recognise true Frenchmen today: by the way they weep, by the way they weep for unhappy, ravaged France. Those who still ask questions while the Boches are in Paris are not men.'

All eyes were on him. Costa had become the sole object of interest. He sensed it and was delighted.

'I know that later there will be people who will treat us as madmen,' he went on. 'None of us know the fate of our country and we are taking up the cudgels for her. But our ignorance is our strength, gentlemen, it stops us hesitating. As far as I am concerned – I have made my choice . . . I prefer to be treated as a madman than as a coward; I'm going on with the war.'

Any other man, purple in the face, clenching his glass, a forest of black hairs emerging from his tennis shirt, might have appeared ridiculous. But emphasis suited Costa; it made him look like an angry, courageous cockerel. Beneath the intentional triteness of his language, one felt genuine passion rumbling like a flow of lava. In turn he had managed to disturb, awaken, captivate, and finally electrify his audience.

In the meanwhile some sailors had approached the ports. Among them were stokers in overalls, Arabs and half-naked Negroes. From minute to minute, their behaviour grew more arrogant. Several of them glued their faces to the glass. The mess room was under observation like the interior of an aquarium. Costa knew it. He beckoned to the second engineer, who was seated not far from him. The man nodded. The guests began to feel nervous and automatically lowered their voices. They felt that there was mutiny in the air. Costa did not wait for it to start. At the top of his voice he continued his diatribe:

'Well, gentlemen . . . Are there any among you who feel inclined to replace the traitors I had to chase off my ship? One only fights well in a clean ship after one has got rid of its vermin and the bilge.'

Soigne realized that the lieutenant was mustering his

supporters to try and nip the threatening mutiny in the bud. He was surprised at the indifference displayed by 'Uncle'. A sneering voice rose on his left; it came from the chief engineer, his neighbour:

'Say, Costa . . . wouldn't it be better if you told these gentlemen what a bastard you are?'

The insult froze the whole company. Costa received it like a blow in the face. He hedged as though trying to avoid a stupid quarrel after too many drinks. Turning to the Belgians, he asked: 'Who's coming to England with me?'

The chief engineer gave him no chance. With the feigned insistence of a drunkard he repeated his insult without changing a syllable: 'Say, Costa . . . wouldn't it be better if you told these gentlemen what a bastard you are?'

This time Costa was obliged to react. For an instant, while the shapes on the deck drew closer, he seemed to hesitate. Was he afraid of some shameful revelation, or was he putting off the painful moment when he would have to lose one of his last mates? No one thought of cowardice when in a more gentle voice he ordered:

'Keep quiet, Marais. If you have something against me, come and see me later in my cabin. I've never been one to avoid an explanation.'

It was too late. The die had been cast – Marais's intentions could be read in his smile. It was a public affront, staged with the connivance of the crew to eliminate Costa. The latter, whispering into the ear of the second engineer, gave his orders. The men outside were taking counsel; obviously there was some hesitation. Tempers were rising in both camps and everyone realized that the fate of the vessel was being decided. The woman could hardly conceal her excitement. The captain, quite impassive, poured brandy into his cup of lukewarm coffee.

Marais clutched his glass, then emptied it in one gulp as though to indicate that a scrap was now inevitable.

'Costa is a rogue,' he said, 'a dirty little rogue who thinks he's

16

a Napoleon. He is trying to take advantage of the circumstances to seize the *Le Rhône*. Look what he's done to Captain Passementton. Yes, it's he who organized the Las Palmas affair. The only thing he didn't tell you is how much it brought him in. Tell them how much you made, Costa. You won't say, eh? You were more communicative a month ago, if you remember. You said that after that coup we should be rolling in money. Who do you think you're kidding? You kept all the dough for yourself.'

A dark flush appeared on the accused man's face. The engineer continued on in the hoarse voice of the drunkard whose obstinacy he was imitating:

'Give me what you promised, Costa. You cheated us all. You diverted the *Le Rhône* off her true course to deliver her to the British. You're no sailor, Costa; you're no hero; you're a filthy little swine. Come on then, give me what you promised.'

Costa was trembling. With a swift movement, he swept the glasses and plates off the table in front of him. He brandished his fist threateningly at the engineer.

'I promised you one thing – that if you ever betrayed me I'd kill you, and that's what I'm going to do now.'

With the surprising agility of small, stocky men, Costa jumped over the table and landed in the middle of the horseshoe. There, he steadied himself and leapt forward. From this point everything went so quickly that no one had time to interfere. Marais broke the stem of his glass on the edge of the table – a glass flower with jagged petals glittered in his hand. He plunged it savagely into his opponent's face.

'You've put my eye out!' screamed Costa. 'I'll get you for that, you traitor!'

The two panting men rolled on the ground among the swivel chairs. Breathing heavily, the Corsican brushed away the sticky liquid which was blinding him with the back of his hand, at the same time striking with cunning savagery, with intent to hurt, to break and to maim. Two of the Belgian officers caught hold of the struggling men in an attempt to separate them. In the midst of the hubbub Captain Passementton tried to regain a little of his lost authority.

'Come, gentlemen,' he cried, 'behave like men.'

A few sailors had come into the mess room, taking advantage of the disturbance. Pale and silent, the woman puffed at her cigarette. Separated and now firmly pinioned by the arms, Costa and Marais faced each other. It was obvious that they represented the two dissenting camps in the *Le Rhône*. The Corsican's face was a single open wound. The engineer was writhing with a broken ankle. The lieutenant lost complete control of himself: 'Put that man in irons!' he roared.

Despite his fury he tried to make a spectacular gesture. A fantastic idea ran through his head. Half-blinded, streaming with blood, his shirt sticking to his skin, red trickles running down his hairy legs, he jerked his chin in the direction of his adversary and thundered:

'I demote you.'

This was the crazy end of a mean little brawl and yet it completely restored Costa's authority. The fratricidal quarrel which had divided the crew of the *Le Rhône* and which later would make one part of France rise against the other, was on this occasion solved merely by force. The new arrivals had chosen. Their adherence carried the sailors with them. Spontaneously two of them offered their services to the lieutenant. The latter repeated his order: 'Put him in irons, near the boiler.'

Costa was shivering. His fingers and his face were bleeding profusely. Soigne went over to him. 'You can't stay like that,' he said, 'we must stop the bleeding.'

Costa turned round abruptly: 'Are you a quack?'

'Yes.'

'Well, see if that sod's cost me an eye and sew up the rest of the damage.'

'Here?'

'In my cabin.'

Dragging his injured leg, Marais roared: 'I'll get you for this, Costa, I'll get you.'

'Are you there, Uncle?' asked the half-blinded lieutenant. 'Good; in half-an-hour pipe everyone down to the hold. You'll march all those cowards past the traitor; I want them to know what to expect.'

Passementton put on his cap, removed his cheroot to the other corner of his mouth and remarked, before leaving the messroom:

'O.K. . . . But you'd do better to get yourself patched up.'

Costa seized Soigne by the arm.

'You're the quack, aren't you? Help me to my cabin. I can't see a thing.'

The woman was at his side; he sensed her presence and his voice softened.

'Ah, there you are. Do you think he's done me?'

The wounded man was helped from the mess room. The deck was already in darkness. A few hundred yards from the *Le Rhône*, a launch was sailing with all lights extinguished; her wake lapped against the hull. There was a tang of brine in the air. 'Does it hurt?' asked Madeleine Guesclin.

Costa shrugged his shoulders. 'No, I'm fine.'

As soon as he was in his bunk, Soigne washed his face and cleaned it with lint and hot water. Costa said nothing, but when the wound was at last visible he asked anxiously: 'Did he get my eye?'

'No, it's unharmed.'

'Well, that's all right, then.'

There were four cuts, one on the forehead, one on the nostril and two on the cheek. The one near the lower eyelid was a deep gash. The blood continued to flow regularly from it. Tight-lipped, Madeleine Guesclin helped Soigne. Her white blouse was bloodstained all down the front. In silence, the Belgian began to put in the stitches. When he started on the lower wound, Costa growled and the doctor thought that he was groaning.

'It won't take long,' he said kindly.

But the patient merely swore between his teeth. 'The bastard, after all I've done for him. But he'll pay dearly for it.'

The girl did her best to quieten him by running her cool hands over his bleeding forehead. Mechanically she scratched off the little black scales of congealed blood which had formed at the roots of the hair. Soigne stood up straight. He was in a muck sweat.

'Where can I wash my hands?' he asked.

The water from the tap spouted into the narrow basin and spattered the cabin wall. Madeleine Guesclin stood up. Nervous anxiety had made her face haggard and drawn. She brought out a bottle of brandy and three glasses, wiping them with the loving care of a hostess. Soigne noticed the banality of her gesture. The patch of blood as it soaked into her blouse outlined one of her nipples in an embarrassing manner. She paid no heed to it. As soon as she had finished wiping the glasses, she placed them on the little table next to the bunk and lit a cigarette. Soigne rinsed his arms up to the elbows. Costa turned to the girl: 'You can make yourself scarce, *mon petit.* We've got things to discuss.'

She left the cabin without a word.

Costa burst into tears. Huddled on his bunk, his face in the dark, he gave way to his nerves. It was a purely physical breakdown and the attack did not last long. The wounded man opened the drawer. It was full of Spanish cigarettes, sealed up at both ends and stuffed with black tobacco. Costa handed one to Soigne and asked: 'I suppose you wonder what sort of a spot you've hit on, eh?'

Soigne was still suspicious. Everything urged him to succumb to Costa's animal magnetism and warlike ardour, but he considered the game too important for it to be played without some reflections. It was a question of throwing in his lot with this man and, once he had made up his mind, there would be no going back on it. He rolled a cigarette between his fingers and lit a match. The strong tobacco filled his lungs and made him blink.

'Captain, at this moment there is a man in pain at the bottom of the hold. I must ask your permission to go and treat him.'

Forgetting his injuries, Costa blew the smoke through his nostrils; a fit of coughing made him double up in bed. Soigne watched him, convinced that he was taking advantage of his discomfort to think out a reply.

The Corsican must have known that the final adherence of the Belgian officer depended on his behaviour. As though unable to control his anger, he growled: 'Let him croak, he's a traitor!'

Possibly it was only a feigned outburst designed to enhance the value of the permission he was about to give. Costa sacrificed a pawn to pursue his attack on the queen. Viciously stubbing out his cigarette in the ashtray, he made a sweeping gesture: 'Bloody tobacco, bloody country, bloody war!' . . .

The Belgian was not deceived. He knew that his adversary was setting a trap, but since he had already decided to capitulate, he was pleased. Costa turned his back on him.

'Go and treat the sod and then come back to me.'

At the door Soigne ran into Passementton. The old sailor had just come up from the stifling hold. He pushed his cap on the back of his head and his forehead was gleaming with sweat.

'Well, that's that,' he said. 'Marais is in irons and the crew is waiting in the hold.'

The wounded man jumped out of bed: 'I'm coming.'

The three men went out on deck. It was dark. Called to order by the captain, the Belgian put out his cigarette. All this excitement had made him forget the defence regulations. When they reached the companion ladder leading to the bowels of the ship, Passementton made way for the lieutenant. A wave of heat rose from the well; the odour, a mixture of paint, tar and spices, caught them by the throat. The crew was assembled below. Costa walked over to his enemy. The sailors were silent. The dim lighting gave an extraordinary brutality to the scene. On the one side Marais, groaning, chained by his ankles and wrists like a trussed hen to a metal stanchion against the bulkhead, on the other, Costa, wearing a blood-stained bandage, a gleam of cruelty in his uninjured eye.

The lieutenant came to a halt a couple of steps from the prisoner: 'Engineer Lieutenant Marais,' he said, 'you have stained your honour, sullied the flag of your ship, and raised your hand against your superiors. I demote you.'

With a swift movement, he tore the stripes from Marais' shoulders, looked in vain for some other insignia of command on his shirt and suddenly caught sight of his cap. He hesitated for a second, then seized it, went over to a port, and with a dramatic gesture flung it into the sea.

'There, my fine fellow,' he said. 'That is what awaits the first man who tries to imitate this scum.' He turned to the doctor: 'He's all yours. Do what you like with him.'

Soigne regained his cabin at about two o'clock in the morning. He opened the door and switched on the light. Brinchant, in the upper bunk, disturbed by the light, growled and turned his face to the wall.

The doctor could not sleep. He felt that he had just made a contact essential to his existence. Everything seemed familiar in this unusual ship, exactly as if his place had already been prepared a long time before.

The previous evening, below decks in the collier, he had been worrying about his fate. Now he knew that his future was no longer in his own hands. It depended on Costa. Soigne smiled to himself in the darkness: Costa – was it the flame of patriotism alone which burned in him? He behaved as though he wanted to commandeer the ship and rule it like a despot. He had already supplanted the vacillating captain, put a recalcitrant officer in irons and installed a woman on board.

Soigne recalled the accusations made by Marais while he was putting his broken ankle in a splint. 'He's a maniac. He's sworn to bend us all to his will and to lead us all to our death. You'll see, he'll suggest stuffing the ship with TNT and sailing her into Kiel to explode in the middle of the German fleet.'

Soigne tossed and turned in his bunk. The heat prevented him from sleeping. The more he thought of it, the more congenial he found the idea of an old tramp steamer, stuffed with TNT, going up in flames among the German warships. . . .

CHAPTER TWO

MUTINY

Costa had said: 'One only fights well in a clean ship.' The following morning as he came out of his cabin, Soigne observed that the slogan had been obeyed to the letter. A team of sailors was swabbing down the deck. He hurried to the messroom. Blaise, in shirt sleeves, a white apron round his waist, was washing the wooden table on which the glasses had left damp circles. For one minute the Belgian thought he was back in his favourite little café in Spa, at opening time. The sun was shining and the square was deserted. The proprietor usually brought him a coffee and a little jug of cream and displayed his interest by asking a question: 'Well, doctor, how goes it? Off on your rounds already?'

The steward saluted the Belgian officer. He waited until he was on the other side of the swinging door which separated the messroom from the galley, before asking: 'A coffee, sir?'

'Yes, and a roll,' replied Soigne.

Nothing intimated that the cabin had been the scene of a fight the previous evening. The *Le Rhône* was a peaceful cargo vessel once more, waiting to sail. Orders were shouted from the bridge, and from the gangways he could hear the complicated noises of a ship's routine. Soigne was not yet accustomed to this permanent hustle of a ship at anchor, which resembles the gurgling of a tall, recumbent body. When Blaise served his breakfast, he thanked him with a nod and asked: 'Has Lieutenant Costa put in an appearance yet?'

'Oh, yes sir, he left a long time ago!' the steward replied. 'He took the launch at eight o'clock and gave orders that we were to eat without him.'

With a gesture of his chin he indicated the activity on deck.

'The decks have to be holystoned for the Admiral's visit.'

'The Admiral?'

'Yes, Muselier. He's coming aboard at three o'clock.'

Soigne began to butter his roll. He heard fragments of a conversation. It came from behind the bulwark at the entrance to the companionway. He recognized the voices of Passementton and Madeleine Guesclin, but not the third – a young Southern voice which sang the words instead of pronouncing them.

'Lieutenant Costa said "It's up to you to choose".'

'And what have you decided, boy?'

There was a silence. The boy must have been hesitating. At last he said: 'Captain, I'm at your service. I'll do whatever you say.'

Soigne pitied Passementton for having to make up his mind, but Madeleine Guesclin interrupted:

'No, this poor lad must go home. You don't want to embroil him in this adventure, do you?'

The old sailor coughed, blew his nose and finally evaded the issue. 'In the present circumstances, nothing forces him to stay or to go. All those who wanted to return to France have been taken ashore by Lieutenant Costa. As far as I am concerned, there can be no hesitation; the Company entrusted the *Le Rhône* to me and I shall stay with my ship to the end.'

The girl, more practical, turned to the ship's boy.

'You know that if you come with us, you may never see your parents again? The war can last for years and the *Le Rhône* will be sent on dangerous missions. How old are you?'

The boy blinked back a few tears and said, with sudden authority in his voice: 'Well, since it's like that ... I'll go home.'

The three walked away along the deck. It was exactly like a station platform at the moment of farewell, at that moment when, despite the bonds that unite them, people split into two elementary groups – those who remain and those who leave.

The doctor rummaged in his pockets, took out his few remaining cigarettes and lit one. The crumpled red and yellow packet with the mark 'Belga' suddenly reminded him of his lost country and his own plight. He wanted to be alone to think things out. Blaise, who was humming as he washed the cups, disturbed him. He left the mess.

The sun beat down on Gibraltar. Main Street, sweltering in the heat, was deserted. Everywhere people were looking for some shade. Even the little shoeblacks had retired to the patches of warmth at the corner of the main street and the stairs. The Indian bazaars were asleep. In the port, however, the rating on duty in front of the Admiralty building continued to stand guard, with his rifle grounded. He was probably thinking of the green flowered meadows of England in June. He caught sight of the stranger, a white bandage around his forehead, walking in the middle of the road as though he had nothing to fear from the sun. At a quick pace he crossed the wooden gangway and the barrier of barbed wire and, saluting the sentry as he passed, made his way into the main hall.

Silence reigned in the Admiralty. Seated behind his desk, Lt.-Commander Brown was going through his files. Automatically he read the slip which the rating handed him and motioned the man to show the visitor in. The electric fan on a cupboard whirred like an imprisoned fly. Brown imagined that he would have to deal with some routine formality. Every morning new boats arriving from the French ports put in at Gibraltar and the British authorities checked their identity and cargoes before allowing them to enter the inner harbour.

The slip bore the following hastily scrawled words:

Lt. Costa from the cargo vessel *Le Rhône*.

'Show him in,' ordered Brown.

Costa was short, sun-tanned and muscular; his white colonial shorts stressed his athletic physique. Brown noticed the bandage. Costa saluted smartly and, without waiting to be asked, sat down on a chair in front of the desk.

'I have come to place my ship, sir' . . . he began in French.

Brown stopped him: 'Do you speak English?'

'No. I'm second mate of the *Le Rhône* which arrived in Gibraltar on the 20th June. I have come to place my ship at the disposal of the Admiralty to defend the port.'

'Cruiser, sloop, destroyer?'

Costa shook his head vigorously.

'Armed merchant vessel with one 100mm, two 20mm cannon and several machine-guns.'

The Englishman took a well-sharpened pencil and pulled his pad towards him.

'The *Le Rhône* you said. Where is she berthed?'

'At the head of the roads.'

'Cargo?'

'Trumpery goods for Senegal. On leaving Marseilles I took on two trucks, a small brake, a car and a consignment of bicycles.'

'Captain's name?'

'Passementton. Two s's and two t's. A double chin.'

The Englishman did not even bother to smile at the joke.

'I'll send an officer on board.'

Costa smiled with the self-assurance of a victorious wild beast.

'No, you'll come yourself tomorrow. For two reasons. Firstly, the war won't wait, and secondly, the *Le Rhône* is the only place in Gibraltar where you can get a decent meal.'

He stood up with a sly look in his undamaged eye and pointed to the door behind Brown.

'Mention me to Admiral Somerville. You'll see that he'll approve.'

Before leaving he saluted once more and gave another smile. Brown watched the door close, noticed the cigarette he had left to burn out in the ashtray and shrugged his shoulders. In due course he would ask the admiral about this fantastic Frenchman who was ready to defend Gibraltar with one 100mm and two 20mm cannon.

At two o'clock Costa returned to his ship. His dressing had been changed and he seemed in a very good temper.

'Does it hurt?' asked Soigne.

'Oh, I've other things to think about,' he said, turning to the captain who was sponging his forehead: 'Uncle, the admiral's coming to see us. He must see the *Le Rhône* looking at her best.'

Passementton shrugged his shoulders.

'Everything's shipshape.'

Costa turned to the Belgian officer: 'Be good enough to come to my cabin.'

Soigne was expecting an explanation but Costa's poise surprised him. The Corsican seemed more self-assured and calmer than he had been the previous evening. Regaining control of the ship and the departure of Marais and the turncoats may be the explanation for this increased confidence, he thought. A psychologist by profession, Soigne considered that Costa must have received some important co-operation while he had been ashore. He wondered about the nature of this and how he had obtained it. So many questions which might or might not be answered.

As soon as the door closed, the injured man offered his visitor the only chair and sat down on his bunk.

'Well, *mon vieux*, my little scrap last night with Marais did not give me time to explain to you a certain number of essential facts. Today order has been re-established in the ship and I intend to put to sea as soon as possible. Destination – England.'

While he spoke, Costa perused the documents he had taken out of his briefcase. Soigne was not hoodwinked. This pre-occupation allowed the lieutenant to keep his eyes lowered.

'Final object of the operation . . .'

Costa looked up: 'Object of the operation? Well, that's the one thing I'm not allowed to tell you. If you want to follow me, you'll have to make the decision blind. All I can assure you is that the *Le Rhône* will get herself talked about and that we shan't waste our time. I need a quack on board. What about it?'

Soigne had been thinking. He knew what he wanted to do, or rather what he did not want to do.

'I crossed the Yser bridges to fight, sir, not to look after the sick. You're French – I'm Belgian. Neither of us know what fate awaits us in England. Apparently there's a Free French Committee over there, so I suppose you'll be joining it.'

'Not on your life.' Costa had put down his papers. 'I know what those military bureaucrats are like. The Free French will wage war in London and their battle campaigns will primarily be concerned with their own promotion. They'll devour each other. I just don't want to meet them. Do you know what I came to do here? According to some people I was bringing a message from Darlan to Muselier and Pétain's betrayal made me change my tack. According to others I am a braggart or an unscrupulous rogue. I can imagine what Marais said to you about the Las Palmas affair. Don't expect me to help you come to a conclusion. The truth is I came to this ship with special operational orders and I shall never relinquish my command. I offer you a war to the death by every possible means, under a borrowed nationality. I can't possibly tell you any more.'

Soigne refrained from mentioning that Marais had not even referred to the Las Palmas affair.

'It's okay with me,' he replied, 'but I don't want to fight as a doctor.'

Costa lit a cigarette and shrugged his shoulders.

'We'll rig up a sick bay for you in case of emergency, but you'll be handling dynamite more often than aspirin. Is that all right?'

Soigne held out his hand. 'I'm with you, captain.'

The ship's boy was weeping. The crew was paraded on the port side; on the starboard side the Belgian officers were standing to attention. On the upper deck, Admiral Muselier, Captain Passementton and Lt. Costa did the honours. The tricolour was hoisted. France was back in the war.

Soigne looked at Costa. Pale, his face heavily bandaged, the lieutenant was trembling with emotion. When they met later in the mess to drink a toast to final victory, he came up to the doctor.

'I owed that gesture to France,' he said. 'Now, until the end of the war, until there's not a single Boche left in Paris, I'm fighting under the British flag.'

Madeleine Guesclin was at the reception, and drank a glass of champagne with the admiral. Soigne decided that she must be Costa's mistress, but nothing in their behaviour warranted this supposition. The Belgian admired the exceptional skill of the injured man who, in one day, after successfully eliminating his adversaries and replacing them at a moment's notice, offered himself the luxury of joining the Royal Navy and of running up the national colours before an admiral whom he did not propose to join.

Life gradually settled down on board. Soigne became Costa's second officer and looked after the fluctuating personnel, recruited today, abandoned the next, according to the arrivals and departures of ships. A sea-going liner from the Far East furnished an important contingent including a regular officer named Grillo, a few genuine sailors, an engineer and a new ship's boy. On the other hand, the *Lieutenant-de-Vaisseau La Tour* left Gibraltar for Oran, carrying the men from *Le Rhône* who had chosen to return to France. In order to avoid any hostile manifestations, her captain had ordered the passengers below until they left the roadstead. That morning, an artificially deserted vessel passed within a few cables length of the *Le Rhône*. Two contending Frances turned their backs on each other.

Soigne very nearly found himself aboard the departing ship. Learning that some Belgian airmen, held up in Oujda, were trying to make Gibraltar, Costa had decided to send them an envoy to arrange a meeting on the African coast. Soigne had volunteered for the mission but Costa was reluctant to part with his second in command. Finally the doctor and another Belgian officer threw dice for the job and the latter embarked in the *Lieutenant-de-Vaisseau La Tour*.

The second mate continued with his task of organization. Most of the volunteers who had joined *Le Rhône* had left France in a hurry without a stitch to their back. To clothe and feed them the holds were systematically ransacked. This was a major operation. A few sailors hollowed out a chimney in the cargo and the most agile of them descended below with a miner's lamp. A dialogue then took place between the speleologist and Soigne aloft with his bills of lading.

'Normally you should find a consignment of men's shirts. Take a good look. The bales are marked DK. They were going to Dakar . . .'

'There are only crates, sir. They weigh at least 80lbs.'

'Hoist one up.'

The crate was passed up and ripped open as soon as it reached the top of the hatch. The contents were never what they expected. Chests in which they hoped to find clothes were full of sugar wrapped up in dark blue paper, starred packets of chicory or chests of China tea. Soigne took a note of everything and distributed the shorts and the shirts in dozens direct to the men. The provisions and the wines went to swell the galley stocks.

With his new recruits and those who had remained faithful,

Costa had formed a crew and a command. Of the old staff, in addition to Passementton, remained Patte, Marais' assistant in the engine room and the lieutenant's trusted man. He was the only one who knew that the *Le Rhône* had slipped away from the convoy on the high seas and made for Gibraltar. The newcomers consisted of the Belgians Soigne and Brinchant, the deserters from the sea-going liner and a few airmen, including Bernard, a refugee from Casablanca. With the exception of Grillo, these men had one thing in common – their complete ignorance of all things nautical. Costa boasted: 'It is the most wonderful command of my career – not a single matelot!'

For all these men the *Le Rhône* meant their last chance. Moored not far from the quay, the cargo represented a haven and a nationality. Thanks to the old deck planking these exiles who had come from Liège, Clermont-Ferrand or Rabat still possessed a country; they would not be delivered naked to the dubious hospitality of Britain in wartime. They would be spared administrative formalities and interrogations. At least Costa assured them of this, and against all reason they believed him. On the ship their wounded patriotism and dismay found a material and moral comfort. Bathed, changed and given food to eat the emigrants became men once more. The doors of great adventure yawned ahead of them.

'We shall fight tooth and nail,' promised Costa.

In the midst of all this excitement, Passementton remained quite calm. An old salt who had sailed round the Horn, he had seen a great deal during his time in sailing ships. Dressed in his old knitted sweater – Costa called it 'his mosquito net' – he sweated comfortably under his cap, a glass of *pastis* always within reach and the moist end of a cheroot between his lips. He dreamed perhaps of the fine day when the *Le Rhône* would return to La Joliette with her cargo of caroubs and cocoa beans as she had always done in the old days. The harbour pilot would come aboard and he would be given a drink. While the tug went about its work arrangements would be made with the

Customs to let through the traditional trash without hindrance. Afterwards there would be long sessions at the Company's Head Office, calculations as to his pension, games of *belote* in the Bar Jean, and endless discussion with Madame Passementton. They called each other '*Mon Doudet*' and they loved each other.

The old sailor knew where his wife kept the gugglet, wrapped up in damp cloths like an unfinished statue; where she hid the felt slippers to be put on before going into the dining room with the highly polished floor. Each thing had its place in this little two-storeyed apartment behind the Vieux-Port. What was he doing in Gibraltar under the orders of an amateur sailor who was ready for any adventure? He had said to the ship's boy before he left: 'The Company entrusted the *Le Rhône* to me and I shall stay with my ship to the end.'

One morning an aircraft which had escaped from North Africa flew over the roadstead. From the bridge of the *Le Rhône* its tricolour circles could be seen quite clearly. The aircraft behaved like a moth fluttering round a lamp. Obviously the pilot was looking for somewhere to land. He finally decided to come down in the sea with his undercarriage retracted.

'Lower a boat!' roared Costa.

Two sailors hurriedly lowered the launch and steamed off in the direction of the shipwrecked aircraft. They brought back two dripping wet airmen, delighted to have got away with it and surprised to find themselves on a French ship.

'Now I'm no longer content to shanghai them off ships. I fish them out of the drink,' said Costa with jubilation.

The following week another aircraft flew in. Less fortunate than its predecessor, it flew over Spanish territory where the ack-ack took it for a target. It was hit, danced about the sky for a moment and then fell seawards. At the end of its fall it caught fire and plunged with its four occupants into the water.

Headed by their captain, the crew of the *Le Rhône*, which

had been given special shore-leave, followed the funeral of the four Frenchmen.

It was very hot and the church smelled of wax. A few Spanish women dressed in black with pale emaciated faces stood against the pillars; soldiers of all nationalities filled the nave. After the funeral the crew of the *Le Rhône* had to return to their ship without taking a turn on the Rock.

'If they're only going to let us ashore for funerals, it's going to be gay,' remarked Bernard.

On the morning of 4th July there was great news in Gibraltar. The Mers-el-Kebir squadron had just been destroyed by Admiral Somerville's guns. Passementton's sailor heart grieved. Costa could not contain his anger.

'Brown will pay for that.'

Soigne thought that the lieutenant shared Passementton's grief and disapproved. He was wrong. Costa was furious with the Englishman for not having allowed him to participate in this mission as he had proposed.

'And to think I stood him a lunch that would have been worthy of Pantagruel!' he roared.

Soigne listened to him with surprise. A great deal separated him from Costa. He was a man from the North, a practitioner, while Costa was a Southerner, a man of action. Moreover, as the days passed he discovered in the Corsican a strangeness and a lack of proportion which both disturbed and fascinated him. Did Costa burn with the flame of fanaticism, with that pitiless and purifying flame which had once ravaged the south of France, driven the Cathari to their destruction and the stake of Monserrat? Did he burn with that fire which a few centuries later had split France in two during the religious wars, plunged her into the most terrible civil war of all?

Perhaps it was that. Today Costa was not afraid to see perish – if possible by his own hand – Frenchmen who did not love France with the same love as his own. An exacting and terrible

34

love which preferred the destruction of the object of his love to the least partition.

Or was he only a humbug of genius who, profiting by the troubled period where nothing counted any more, when all values had vanished in the collapse of a world, had seized the opportunity of living a picturesque life?

Or, more simply, was Costa scouring the country and Marais was right?

Inaction maddened this volcanic, hot-blooded creature. Having exchanged his bandage for an elastoplast dressing, he no longer shaved. A stubbly grizzled beard covered his face. It outlined the other scar on his cheek, the one due to a bullet – a bullet which in moments of irritation he still seemed to be chewing between his teeth. Everything irritated him – an interruption at table, the soup when it was too hot, or an unpolished brass rail. The crew lived in a state of perpetual anxiety. Even the Arab stokers complained. One evening, unable to contain himself any longer, Soigne decided to pay him a visit. He found him poring over a huge atlas.

'Ah, it's you, quack,' said the lieutenant. 'Come and look at this.'

He was very excited. With one finger he pointed to a spot on the chart in the neighbourhood of Tortuga Island.

'If those English beggars don't give satisfaction in a week, I shall slip out at night under their noses. I'll set a course for the West Indies and we'll work on our own account.'

Costa's impatience was largely caused by the dilatoriness shown by three British officers to whom Brown had sent him in despair. Tossed about like a tennis ball between these three supposed protectors, the Corsican felt the moment coming when, in his own words, 'he would feed one of them to the fishes.' He could not understand why the Admiralty, busy as it was, should not give the fate of his ship priority. Waiting for a decision he evolved the craziest plans.

One morning he ordered the launch and returned to his

cabin. A few minutes later he came out, newly shaved and carrying a suitcase stuffed to bursting point. From the rails Brinchant, Soigne and Bernard watched him leave.

'Where's he off to?' asked Brinchant.

'To post his mail perhaps,' said the doctor, with a shrug of the shoulders.

Bernard wrinkled his nose and with downcast eyes chuckled to himself.

'In any case, I'd like a little trip ashore myself . . .'

The young airman had made himself famous during the only evening he had spent without leave in Gib. That evening Grillo had lent him his uniform and the pilot, happy to feel the pavement under his feet, had joined forces with some officers from the *Ark Royal* on shore leave. He did not reappear until two o'clock in the morning. Riding a cab-horse, he politely asked the way from a sentry posted at the end of the quay. A British lieutenant had replaced the coachman. The latter, even more drunk than his passengers, was sleeping quite peacefully inside his cab. Bernard had wrapped him up tenderly in a blanket.

Brown sighed when he saw Costa come in. What fantastic new proposal had he brought? The Englishman preserved his normal calm. If Costa had suggested a trip to Hamburg in the *Le Rhône*, followed by the kidnapping of Hitler in the middle of Berlin by a suicide commando, he would merely have replied 'I'll mention the matter to Admiral Somerville.'

The Frenchman sat down and ostentatiously laid his brief-case on the desk. Brown remarked politely that it was very full. Clutching onto the leather handle, Costa agreed.

'Well, what's new?'

The visitor seemed quite relaxed.

'I owe you an apology. The day before yesterday I told you that your three colleagues were no good. I was wrong.'

The Englishman was about to make some amiable reply

when the lieutenant interrupted 'I know when I'm wrong. They are good for something – they're good enough to hang!'

Brown could not prevent giving a start. Pretending to ignore it, Costa went on in the same elegant, worldly tone:

'If I were their chief, I would send them before a court martial for deliberately sabotaging the war effort. But since I'm not their chief,' the Corsican smiled and brought from his brief-case three parcels wrapped up in chestnut-coloured paper, each bearing a label . . . 'I have merely brought each of them a present.'

Brown sighed with relief. This was obviously a rather dubious Continental joke and the Frenchman was trying to get round his allies by delving into the gastronomic reserves of the *Le Rhône*.

For form's sake he protested. 'They're only doing their duty.'

Costa stood up and the clasps of his briefcase snapped open.

'I'll leave you the parcels and ask you to have them delivered to their respective offices.'

Standing up behind his desk, Brown said 'I'll see to it personally.'

Everything seemed to have been arranged amicably. Before leaving, however, the Corsican bared his pointed teeth and added: 'And don't wait too long. They're delayed-action bombs!'

The door banged.

Only then did the Englishman notice the regular ticking in the three little packages.

Costa knew the exact limits to which he could go and his supreme skill consisted in knowing how to choose the moment when he had to go too far.

After he had left, Brown rushed into Admiral Somerville's office while an artificer, summoned in haste, rendered the bombs harmless in the cellar. The conversation between these two officers was brief and decisive.

'The *Le Rhône* will leave with the next convoy for England. She will fly the British merchant navy flag.'

Costa had won. This victory could not be attributed to the affair of the bombs, which would merely have infuriated the Admiralty and rendered the lieutenant who had been guilty of the gesture liable to imprisonment. But other considerations known to Admiral Somerville after he had received a cable from London, had intervened in favour of this disturber of the peace.

The naval intelligence service had indicated in a most peremptory manner that Costa was a reliable man and that he was to be given satisfaction. The Corsican had only decided to take the big gamble knowing that he was well within his rights. His outburst marked the conclusion of his secret contacts taken on the Rock behind the Admiralty's back. As soon as he had arrived at Gibraltar, he had reported to the Chief of the French Naval Mission.

'Put me in touch with a service intelligence officer,' he requested.

The sailor had been unfavourably impressed by this strange, arrogant officer who pretended to have been entrusted with a special mission by the Minister for the Colonies. He noted on his pad his impressions of the mysterious visitor.

Braggart. Carries an absolute arsenal with him. Patriotism seems sincere. Always talking of his past exploits and of those he is preparing. And in conclusion: I realize that certain operations require special individuals, but here certain energies have to be canalized because, if left to themselves, they sometimes prove more dangerous than useful. Seems to me a fanatic.

The Chief of the French Naval Mission, however, gave him the contact he had asked. Did this new contact justify Costa's hold over the Admiralty? Or should one look for anterior bonds and more secret reasons? The sudden docility of the masters of Gibraltar remained a mystery for the officers of the *Le Rhône* and added to the aura of its strange lieutenant.

CHAPTER THREE

ESCAPE TO FIGHT

The announcement that they would soon be putting to sea had cheered the crew but, after a few days of fruitless waiting, enthusiasm waned.

An Italian raid on the Rock did little to arouse any warlike ardour. The British ack-ack went into action, spangling the sky with black and white blobs of cotton wool. Like harmless butterflies the two reconnaissance aircraft circled at a great height. On the *Le Rhône* Bernard, who had just been promoted gunnery officer, was at his post. Costa could not resist the temptation for long. 'Aim your machine-guns at them when they turn over Spanish territory.'

'They're flying too high.'

'I know that. You'll hit the Algeçiras Barracks.'

After a few expressly clumsy salvoes, the ship ceased fire. Besides, the two Italian planes, having finished their reconnaissance, retired as they had come. The following morning a note arrived from the Admiralty thanking the *Le Rhône* for the aid she had given the harbour defences and begging her captain in future to abstain should similar circumstances arise.

It was hot and the crew, condemned to rest on board, was thoroughly bored. Grillo and Bernard shared a cabin and the former, who had arrived with his packs from the liner, helped his friend out with a few articles of everyday necessity. There was a lack of toothpaste, razor blades and handkerchiefs; the few packets of Players brought back from the town by Costa were a real luxury. In his off-duty hours, Grillo taught the airman the rudiments of maritime navigation, but Bernard busied himself chiefly with the ship's armaments. A workshop had been fitted up for him with the help of Rinto, the gunner's mate, where he could dismantle, oil and reassemble. Rinto, a Parisian fitter, thought of nothing else but taking guns to pieces. He looked at the weapons with a sort of gluttony and kept repeating to try and convince himself: 'The armoury is the antechamber of war.'

Soigne supervised everything: the inventory of the holds, the galley provisions, and the detail of the watches. He, too, dreamed of heroic actions. He planned the formation of a landing commando and skilfully sounded the men with a view to choosing the best. Patte was one of these. He had sailed a great deal, sometimes in thorny circumstances, and nothing surprised him.

'You bet I know the Spanish coast,' he said in his appalling accent. 'I was chief engineer in an old tub which supplied the Republicans with arms and provisions. Talk of a *corrida*! They signalled to us with pieces of red canvas when the coast was clear ...'

He knew tricks, learned in all latitudes, the right haunts in every port, the thousand and one means of defrauding the Customs, and his judgments on the sailors of various nationalities were always prejudiced.

'A Greek owner ... you can't imagine what he's like until you've met one. They have one eye on the cargo and the other on the insurance policy. When the boat's empty, a Greek skipper sets fire to her and collects the insurance.'

Brinchant had been promoted Photographic Officer and assistant to the commando team. This double job delighted Costa, who said: 'He can film our landings and we'll sell them to 20th Century Fox or Movietone News.'

But the time hung heavy on their hands. Passementton was taciturn. He had tried to get a letter through to Marseilles and was eating his heart out waiting for a reply. Madeleine Guesclin never left her cabin except to toast her arms and legs in the sun. She did not seem to worry that she disturbed the already overheated male imaginations on board. As he passed her, Bernard screwed up his eyes as though the light disturbed him and said to Grillo: 'I'm waiting till she's done to a turn.'

Soigne decided to warn Costa.

'Captain, I think we have two alternatives. Either to let the men go ashore or bring some girls aboard.'

'How many do you want?'

Despite his medical training, Soigne was disconcerted; he hesitated a few seconds before replying.

'That depends on the time they'll spend on board.'

Costa did nothing to help him.

'Make out a detailed plan. The number, time spent, the share of expenses between the officers and the ratings. I'll get some gen about the prices in Gibraltar.'

Contrary to all rational forecasts, the business was arranged. The Admiralty, horrified, merely replied: 'We don't want to know.'

Five professionals were engaged and the pinnace was to fetch them early at a certain spot on the quayside. That morning, Costa left the ship with a final recommendation to Soigne: 'See that everything goes off all right.'

The officers and men were seized with a feeling of self-respect. Reduced to a purely hygienic operation, the anticipated pleasure suddenly appeared to them contemptible. After a brief confabulation they all signed off and returned to their normal duties. Costa returned late.

'Well, how did it go?' he asked.

'You see, sir, we did not think we were justified in bringing women on board a ship.'

The Corsican's face lit up. His crew was reacting after his own heart. He wanted it to be independent and at the same time disciplined. A real band of Corsairs; with such men he would accomplish great deeds.

With animal obstinacy, Costa continued his negotiations with the Admiralty. Day after day he squeezed new concessions out of them and made new demands.

'I demand protection of the British flag.'

'Against whom?'

'Against the Free French.'

The Admiralty was in a quandary. It had to respect the agreements made between Churchill and De Gaulle, by which each new Frenchman who rallied to the flag came under the jurisdiction of the London Committee, and, on the other hand, to obey the formal instructions received from England that Costa was to be given satisfaction.

The latter did not hesitate to declare: 'If the Free French try to take my boat they'll burn their fingers. My guns are always loaded and I have armed the crew.'

Brown looked with terror, tinged with admiration, at this enterprising, truculent Corsican, who as second mate on an old French cargo tub wanted to bargain with the Royal Navy as an equal. He began by proposing the Red Ensign, the emblem of the Merchant Navy. Costa replied coarsely: 'You can stick that on the wall.'

He considered that he had a right to the White Ensign, reserved for warships, and developed a paradoxical theory.

'The *Le Rhône* is not a merchant ship; she is an assault craft camouflaged as a cargo vessel.'

Finally they agreed upon the Blue Ensign, the flag of the RNR and, to sweeten Admiral Muselier, it was decided that since the *Le Rhône* was to join one of His Majesty's convoys she was provisionally to fly a British flag. Costa was radiant. Soigne had removed the last stitches and now that he no longer wore a dressing he seemed to take on a new lease of life. This manifested itself in reorganization meetings on board and escapades in Gibraltar. On his return from one of these trips, the Corsican related without a trace of shame how he had seduced the violinist of a woman's orchestra in Main Street. When he proceeded to give a wealth of details without apparently noticing the presence of Madeleine Guesclin, Marcelac, one of the new recruits, a slightly effeminate-looking airman, said tartly: 'Captain, you forget that there is a woman present.' Costa gave a loud guffaw: '*Bon Dieu*, that's true, I didn't notice you.'

Two days after obtaining the Blue Ensign, Costa returned to the Admiralty. Brown was away and he was received by an officer who was very much on his guard. Meticulous and precise, the Corsican insisted upon reviewing his whole case from the beginning in front of this inexperienced official.

'I'm second mate of a ship called *Le Rhône*, which has lain for several weeks in the Gibraltar roads. My vessel flies the Blue Ensign.'

'I see?'

'She comes therefore under His Britannic Majesty's orders.'

'Precisely.'

'That being the case then, I have to see that she respects KR and AI.'

'No shadow of doubt about that.'

'Well, then, I have to bring to your notice a fact unprecedented in the British Navy. Neither my officers nor myself have received our pay.'

Once more audacity paid. The Admiralty was conciliatory. It admitted that men who had arrived on their own initiative in a free port might be destitute. Each of them was to receive from three to five pounds 'advance pay', ten bottles of port and two thousand Spanish cigarettes. From that moment shore leave took on a different aspect. With money in their pockets, Soigne, Brinchant, Bernard, Patte and their mates strolled down Main Street. They ransacked the Indian Bazaar for trash and bargained for the hams, sausages or spiced *sobresades* hanging in the grocers' windows. Laden with parcels, they explored the busy streets and admired the strange sights – Gibraltar cabs, carts piled high with yellow and green melons, sailors on leave, rawboned Highlanders, sellers of lottery tickets and the small shoeblacks quarrelling for customers on the pavement. In the middle of the crowd towered the figure of a London policeman, making the traffic keep to the left. Horns were forbidden and the local buses – real museum pieces – cleaved a passage by shouting '*Pasajé pasajé*!'

Grave and dignified, the sun-tanned conductor leant out of the door and slapped the swaying coachwork to make the pedestrians move out of the way.

At night they invaded the small Spanish cafés in the alleys or in the dark stairways of the Citadel. When they grew tired of the *tipicos*, *flamencos* and *manzanillas*, they moved on to the big establishment in Main Street, famous for its female orchestra. At six o'clock all the Spaniards working on the Rock had to cross the frontier and at eleven o'clock even the dancers left. The evening then continued in cosmopolitan hotels until the arrival of the naval MPs carrying truncheons, who were there to see that the midnight curfew was respected. They returned aboard in an '*Araba*', a kind of oriental, open gharry.

Towards the 15th July, the *Le Rhône* at last received orders to join an England-bound convoy. For the whole crew this departure symbolized a definite break with the past. From now onwards their fate was bound up with that of Costa and they did not yet know what 'great deeds' they were going to accomplish together. Conditions on board were appalling; a hundred and fifty sailors herded in the holds and the officers sharing eight of the passenger cabins. Strict discipline was enforced and the watches were kept regularly. Grillo, the only man apart from Passementton capable of setting a course, served as instructor.

'You see, Bernard, it's quite simple. The convoy is using Code No. 14. At the hour you veer 15° to port, at the quarter you go over to 20°, at three-quarters you return to 15° and at the hour you are back on your original course.'

The sailing orders were constantly changed in order to fox the German U-boats prowling off the French coast. Ahead or astern of the *Le Rhône*, the nearest ships occasionally hove in sight according to visibility. From time to time an escort vessel, like a busy sheepdog, passed the cargo vessel, throwing up a curtain of spray. Thanks to the sun and the sea air the men now looked like old sea dogs. They stressed this even more by growing a beard and putting on the classic roll collar sweater. Soigne had rigged up a small, rudimentary sick bay in which he never set foot. Brinchant took photographs and Bernard spent the hours between watches greasing the weapons which the sea water constantly rusted.

Each man grew accustomed to this peaceful monster which was to serve him as a home and an action station. The *Le Rhône* had an overall length of two hundred and seventy feet and a forty-one foot beam. She was coal driven and her 1,100 hp engine allowed her in theory to do 9·5 knots – in practice she panted like a sick beast above eight knots. For twenty years she had been on the Dakar-Saloum-Casamance run. Later she was seen in the Black Sea and in the Moroccan and Senegalese ports; her log book totalled one hundred and forty voyages. This ancient 'tub' sweated paint from all her rotten timbers. The odour began as soon as the engines started and only disappeared after several days at sea. A mysterious distillation took place in the shivering hull, creating and destroying these miasmas. Patte, who was a bit of a scientist, announced one morning: 'Tomorrow she won't smell any more.' He was right.

Amidships was what used to be called the 'castle' in the age of sail. Passementton affected this obsolete term which must have evoked old memories for him. Atop was the bridge, flanked by two servo-controls, a chart room and a small wireless cabin. A companion ladder descended to the captain's quarters. As a result of Costa's equivocal position, these quarters were divided: Passementton used one cabin while Costa occupied the other next to the saloon and the bathroom. Madeleine Guesclin had a cabin of her own. Wooden steps, always impeccably waxed, led to the mess rooms which were on a level with the main deck. Next to the officers' mess were the engineers' mess, the galley, Blaise's pantry and a ladder leading down to the engine room. From there rose a stench of hot grease mixed with the odours of cooking which caught the throat. To gratify his taste for theatrical gestures Costa had insisted on installing the irons at the bottom of these stifling stairs, just next to the boiler.

'Defaulters will see the stuff I'm made of.'

To port and starboard were rows of cabins and passages painted a dirty grey. Even in calm weather a violent draught the origin of which was never discovered always blew along these passages. They were seldom used. The outside gangways enabled the crew to pass from one end of the ship to the other.

The *Le Rhône* had a tall funnel, two masts and a derrick for handling heavy cargo. Fore and aft Costa had mounted hexagonal platforms, each carrying two twin guns. The deckhands' quarters were forward on the spar-deck and the stokers' quarters aft. Finally, below decks the engines and the four holds. In one of these hammocks had been slung for extra passengers.

The first impression of these amateur sailors recruited in Gibraltar was that a merchant ship made the same demands as an old copper coffee set: it had to be cleaned constantly. The second was that the day did not consist of twenty-four hours as on land, but of three quarters of eight hours. Eventually they realized that there were plenty of distractions. When the *Le Rhône* had to put on speed, Patte called for volunteers to stoke. He worked himself and Brinchard, Bernard and a few airmen turned up, stripped to the waist, shovel in hand. As the coal disappeared into the boiler they roared those famous, obscene songs which, according to pukka sailors, would make a negress blush in the dark. Grillo had a fantastic repertoire. He had chosen the ditties with the care of a well-bred archivist; for him they had a strange, subtle charm. He knew how to discriminate between those for 'hoisting' and those for 'tugging', attaching more importance to the rhythm than to the words. Standing behind the stokers, by the light of the flames, the sweat pouring from his forehead, he took a delight in being a proletarian. After a time his tall shape would be seen climbing the ladders which zigzagged up into the sunlight. When the weather and the boat's position allowed it, Costa allowed them to practise firing depth charges. Bernard was surprised to see white fountains of spray rising a few cables length away from the ship. The demands of the timetable prevented them lowering a boat to collect the miraculous catch they could see gleaming silver among the waves.

For Bernard, weapons were bewitched. He loved their icy contact and the odour of rancid oil they emitted. He would often be found in the magazine with the port wide open, taking a grenade to pieces. He used to bet Rinto that the detonator would explode in the course of his dismantling. He lived in the company of these malevolent beasts, rather like a lion tamer who caresses his new-born cubs.

'You see,' he said to his oppo, 'I was a pilot in Morocco. I had seven hours flying time when the Germans broke through in France. Had I listened to my chiefs I should still be there looking at aircraft stripped of their props and magnetos. But one morning three of us tried to take off in a Glen Martin; we had no luck; we were picked up. I managed to slip away and a few days later I discovered a ship taking on Polish aviators. I pretended to be one of them.'

'How did you work it?'

Bernard screwed up his eyes and pretended to be busy with the detonator.

'Do you know the difference between a Pole who keeps his

47

trap shut and a Frenchman who does the same? No? Well, there isn't any. So, if you slip among a bunch of Polish aviators without saying a word, no one notices you.'

Soigne was busy studying the problem of Costa. By tacit agreement the Belgian was his second in command, but after the perfunctory explanation in Gibraltar, Costa had never divulged any more confidences. He kept out of sight and sometimes two days passed before he came down to the mess. Blaise served him in his cabin. One morning, as they were approaching the Irish coast and the weather was growing worse, the doctor plucked up courage to knock at his cabin door. Costa received him completely naked, in a tiny hip bath. With an overflowing ashtray within reach of his hand he was turning over some old soap-stained magazines. The visitor's entrance did not disturb him.

'Shut the door, *mon vieux*.'

He was smoking his accursed Spanish cigarettes and the smoke and the steam made the air quite unbreathable.

Soigne noticed that Costa's powerful chest was covered with scars. He wondered if there was any part of his flesh that was free of them. One day Brinchant had surprised him putting on his shoes and was horrified to see that the soles of his feet were entirely covered with scarred tissue. The Corsican had burst out laughing.

'Didn't they ever tell you that Chinese cooking was the best in the world? The yellow men know better than anyone how to cook feet in the ashes. They maintain that it makes frank conversation easier.'

Was Costa speaking the truth? If not, where did his lies begin? Soigne had pondered a long time on this subject; by cross-checking and intuition he had managed to detach from its background a figure, the essentials of which, however, still remained unknown quantities. It was obvious that both Costa and Madeleine Guesclin belonged to the French counter-espionage department. Various allusions at meal times seemed to confirm this. They had spent a long time in the Far East and the war must have taken them by surprise in Saigon.

'I speak eight Indo-Chinese dialects fluently,' Costa maintained.

On this point no one could contradict him.

If the young woman was to be believed, the Minister for the Colonies recalled them to Paris at the beginning of 1940; they had attended a sabotage school not far from Vincennes. One name often cropped up – the name of a British liaison officer called Johns. Counter-espionage, special missions, sabotage, all these words possessed a strange power of suggestion for Soigne, whose head was filled with extraordinary adventures. Nevertheless, he was still suspicious. 'It's too good to be true,' he said to himself.

He could not believe that fate had given him such a fabulous appointment in the roads of Gibraltar. And yet, how could the attitude of Passementton be explained unless Costa had come aboard with orders to take over the command? That was an avenue which had to be explored. Soigne sat down near the bath-tub and lit a cigarette. Once more, the Corsican was a step ahead of him.

'I've decided not to call you Soigne any more,' he said. 'It's pretentious for a quack. You ought to have a more warlike name – what about Mortiss?'

The Belgian burst out laughing. 'Mortiss is OK by me,' he said.

Costa moved his legs lazily in the warm water.

'So, Mortiss, you'd like to know who you're dealing with, eh?'

Obviously this devil of a man guessed everything.

'You know, *mon vieux*, when I was a kid I had a marvellous toy. An aluminium motorbike which turned on its own and automatically switched on its headlamps. It was terrific. One day I dismantled and reassembled it completely. It was no longer the same motorbike and sidecar. You should never try and find out what makes things tick. If I told you that I'd strangled two men with my own hands and took a certain delight in it, would you hesitate to follow me?'

'No.'

'Well, tell yourself that I've strangled four and leave me in peace.'

Costa put out his cigarette in the bath water. It floated to the surface. Soigne smiled.

'Since you don't want to tell me anything about yourself, perhaps I had better explain to you how I got to Gibraltar.'

The lieutenant picked up a piece of soap and rubbed his chest energetically.

'That's a good idea. Tell me your life story.'

Soigne related the grievous period of waiting with his unit in front of the Yser. One morning the order came through for the officers and men to lay down their arms before midday: Belgium had capitulated. Soigne refused to accept this decision. He kept his revolver, saluted the Colonel, and with two friends left in a car for France. The troops were disbanded. Rifles were stacked by the roadside like piles of matches. The car had to force a way through groups of infantrymen who looked askance at them. After a while, they met a vehicle flying a white flag – the German plenipotentiaries had arrived to see that the surrender orders were being carried out. Fortunately, it was not quite midday. . . .

'Would you mind soaping my back as you go on?' asked Costa.

After crossing the bridge over the Yser, Soigne entered a new world. The French and the British still did not know of the tragedy which was taking place a few hundred yards away. They still thought that Belgium was at war. An incredulous officer accompanied the three fugitives from HQ to HQ until the news finally came over the radio: 'Belgium has just capitulated.'

This announcement had the effect of a drop of acid on Soigne. It burnt him and at the same time a host of conflicting sentiments began to seethe within him. From now on he had no ties. His fidelity to the King could wait until the end of the war. He managed to embark at Dunkirk for England. A few days later he was back in France. Everywhere he met Belgian officers completely resigned to the defeat. He left them without anger and sought the sole issue possible – in combat.

Costa had just plunged his head under water. It emerged running with water, accompanied by sniffs and sighs. When he had finished shaking himself, he turned towards his visitor.

'You're right, Mortiss,' he said. 'It's no longer worth while being angry with anyone. At first I was all for sending Pétain before a court martial. Now I should be quite pleased to see him made custodian of a public garden – if only to see what a face the London Committee would make.'

CHAPTER FOUR

LETTERS OF MARQUE

On the evening of 16th August, Patte in his wireless operator's cabin picked up a broadcast from the BBC . . . 'This is General de Gaulle speaking.'

The men had gathered round to listen.

'Those who are fighting for victory have a clear conscience and a heart filled with hope, for they know that it will soon be recognized who has betrayed and who is serving France,' said the voice, distorted by the atmospherics.

This speech consoled the sailors who were rather discouraged by wandering about the high seas in a convoy, like dogs kept on a leash. They now knew that the Cameroons, Tchad and French Equatorial Africa had rallied or joined the dissenters according to the different terminologies. A few of them, however, began to have doubts. After succumbing to the collective frenzy in Gibraltar, they were now worried as to their fate and their minds grew heated. Once they arrived in England they would merely be prisoners. If they were to act they would have to do so at once.

One evening Soigne and Lebasque, one of the young air cadets, were on watch together. Neither of them had yet grown accustomed to these long night vigils, interrupted by the incessant changes of course. It was a warm night and the sea so calm that hardly a ripple lapped along the hull. After some minutes Soigne began to feel nervous. On several occasions he had noticed shadows creeping about the deck. The darkness gave them a guilty aspect. The doctor kept his eyes open. Behind him the helmsman did not seem aware of anything. Lebasque was wearing the fixed expression of a young man trying to battle with sleep. Soigne noticed the birthmark on his cheek; it was claret colour and the moonlight made it appear monstrous.

Pity he did not get it treated earlier, thought Soigne. He's a stout fellow and because of this blemish on his face he courts antipathy as others court affection. That patch has changed his life . . .

To stand beside a man for several hours on watch without exchanging a word, observing the progress of a ship, teaches you more about him than any lengthy conversation would do. Sailors are well aware of this and they also know the virtue of a silence shared.

Now there was no possible doubt. Men were walking towards the bridge. Footsteps echoed on the companionway; they sounded like explosions in the silence. There was a threat in these concerted footsteps; no one would have stamped to such an extent had he not been prepared to commit violence.

Three shadows appeared together. Behind the glass of the wheelhouse the man at the helm had not stirred. For a moment Soigne wondered whether he were an accomplice, but the leading sailor was already standing before him. Soigne recognized him: an enormous fellow from Dunkirk who worked in the engine room. He stood there, scowling, legs apart and jaws clenched.

'What's the trouble, boy?'

Soigne automatically had addressed him as he would have addressed an injured worker somewhere in Walloon country. The leader shook his head. He had obviously hesitated a long time and would not beat a retreat now.

'Well, you see, me and my mates don't want to go to England.'

'Have you gone crackers?'

An indistinct growl ran up the companion way. Soigne still tried to avoid the worst.

'You know what you risk if I call the captain?'

'Couldn't care bloody less.'

The proximity of France had had a magnetic effect on these men and had incited them to mutiny. Responsible for sailing a ship in convoy in a dangerous zone, Soigne had to re-establish order without delay.

'Quesnoy – that's your name, isn't it? If you don't return to the hold I shall be forced to tell the captain.'

Quesnoy did not give up. Impassive as a pitprop, anchored in his determination, he expressed himself quite gently. A cold resolution could be felt behind this gentleness.

'If you won't change course, let us leave in a lifeboat with provisions and fresh water; we'll fend for ourselves.'

'Quesnoy, for the last time, I order you to return to the hold.'

'No.'

'All right, then. I'll tell the captain.'

Instinctively the leader of the mutineers approached the Belgian. Soigne looked at the men's hands; they were unarmed. The speaking tube from the bridge led directly to Costa's cabin. For several days, for no official reason, everyone had called the Corsican 'captain'. Passementton did not seem to take it amiss. The *Le Rhône* had two captains, that was all. Quesnoy knew perfectly well to whom Soigne was alluding.

Costa must have been asleep. It needed several calls before his furious voice burst in their ears. 'What's going on?'

'A group of sailors is here on the bridge. They want to be allowed to return to France.'

'What?'

Lebasque did not take his eyes off his course. Unruffled, he gave the order to the helmsman: 'Fifteen degrees starboard fifteen.'

Below in his bunk Costa began to get irritated.

'What are you babbling about, Mortiss. Are you drunk?'

'No, sir. Quesnoy and several of his mates insist upon leaving.'

'Smash the bastards in the teeth.'

'But, sir . . .'

'What you mean, sir? Aren't you ashamed to disturb me because of four drunks? Are you my Jimmy the One or not?'

A scrap, even at unequal odds, did not worry Soigne, but he hated to embark upon one in cold blood. Once more he turned to the man from Dunkirk:

'Quesnoy, go below with your mates. I'll come and see you when my watch is finished.'

The sailor shook his head. 'No, sir, I'm not leaving here.'

Costa was growing impatient.

'Well, Mortiss, have you done it? Yes or no?'

An explosion of rage made the tube vibrate.

'Insubordination, disobedience in wartime, mutiny – what more do you want? For them to give you a baby . . .?'

There was a brief silence and then: 'I'm coming up.'

The catastrophe could not now be avoided. Soigne prayed that Costa was not armed and at the same time feared that the stokers would suddenly produce crowbars. There was the sound of hastening footsteps, then the door of the charthouse opened and Costa came in. He had put on his trousers and flung a tunic over his bare chest. He pushed the Belgian roughly aside and went up to Quesnoy.

'Are you the one that's getting stroppy?'

Without waiting for a reply, he smashed his fist home in the miner's face. He always managed to have the setting of his ring on the top and it drew blood. Quesnoy did not seem to notice the blow. Costa was foaming at the mouth.

'Have you understood now?'

The sailor did not even wipe the cut. He looked at his superior and said in a strangled voice: 'I'll kill you.'

Fortunately, Costa did not hear him. He had already seized the two men next to him and was shaking them.

'Well, what's stopping you from putting this rogue in irons?'

They refused with a shake of the head. The Corsican jostled them and roared at the others who were coming up the companionway: 'I give you thirty seconds to take these three bastards down into the stoke-hole. Then I'll fetch my revolver and I'll fire blind into you all.'

Although he was alone with bare fists and no weapon, he was terrifying. He seemed to possess a charm; without a word the sailors came forward and the three leaders let themselves be taken away. Soigne was completely baffled. If I'd seen that on the films, I shouldn't have believed it, he thought to himself.

As soon as the bridge was clear, Costa turned to Lebasque.

'Don't forget to keep a good course.'

And he returned to his cabin.

August came to a close with a heat wave. The *Le Rhône* entered the mouth of the Bristol Channel like a queen. She was no merchant ship entering the flank of Great Britain during the war, but a vessel carrying a crew of men haunted by questions. This state of mind had evolved once they had sighted the coasts of Ulster and Scotland, and had taken the Northern Channel to reach the Irish Sea. By the time they sighted the Welsh shore, the slate blue cliffs of Caernarvon and the dull red hills of Merionethshire, the men were aware of their sole dependence upon Great Britain. Now they were quite close to the British Isles. After passing the Isle of Man they knew their destination – Barry in the Bristol Channel, the harbour between Swansea and Cardiff. The *Le Rhône* would make port there after taking the schoolboy route to the North, far from the German submarines which haunted the Channel. Once they had anchored and tied up, what would become of this old 'tub' and the men in her? By his forceful coup in the Mediterranean and his intransigent attitude in Gibraltar, Costa had literally delivered the *Le Rhône* to her fate. Never more would she crawl along the African coasts, laden with trash, wine from Sète, tinned goods and pith helmets. Never more would Passementton be on the bridge, his cap over his eyes, cheroot in mouth, bawling at some native pilot half asleep at his work. Never more would the Pharos of Marseilles announce the peaceful arrival of the *Le Rhône* with the notice: 'Expected today.' Presumably she would never again see the immaculate beauty of Frioul, L'Estaque and the Château d'If before entering the Straits of La Joliette on a summer morning. Other adventures awaited her – but what? They would have to land and see. To know what kind of reception the British would give to their unfortunate allies.

On this point the most varied forecasts were bandied about in the officers' mess. Some maintained that every foreigner who landed in England was subjected to interminable interrogations and forced to spend a few weeks in a camp for screening. Others insisted that the British allotted all the minor tasks to the refugees. Sitting on a stool, with lowered head, staring at his cigarette smoke, Bernard shrugged his shoulders.

'We shall see. The main thing is to get ashore.'

Passementton had shaved and put on his dark blue uniform. He looked terribly sad. The previous evening he had confessed to Soigne, whom he had relieved on the bridge: 'It breaks my heart to take my ship into a British port without the French flag.'

The Belgian could not help remembering the famous card game scene in *Marius*, with César's fantastic Provençal quip: 'I tell you, you break my heart!'

But the old sailor's grief was very sincere. His eyes had filled with tears and he had thrown away an unfinished cigarette. Now he said to the officers: 'You'll see, it will be even worse than in Gibraltar; we shan't even be allowed to come alongside.'

Patte, the second engineer, burst out: 'What did you say? The English aren't the bosses – we have people in London to defend us.'

When the *Le Rhône* passed the Swansea lighthouse on its rocky spur, Quesnoy and the two other rebels were still languishing in chains near the boiler. The ship was a prey to conflicting sentiments, from the bridge to the stoke-hole, from fore to aft. Curiosity was the dominating element. They were approaching the old Island, lashed now by the tempest of war, and which for several days had borne the brunt of the Luftwaffe bombing. Everyone was anxious about his immediate future. Apart from Costa's trusty henchmen, the men envisaged being transferred to a fighting unit of their own nationality, where they would fight in their own branch of the service. For many of them the joint adventure seemed to stop here; they already looked upon the *Le Rhône* as a thing of the past, one way of getting to England.

Alone in his cabin Costa behaved as though it were no concern of his. Bernard reported to him a few hours before they entered the roads.

'Have you any particular instructions concerning the weapons, sir?'

He had found him shaving in front of the mirror. Spread out on the bunk was a brand new shirt, a symbol of his love of elegance. Costa turned round, twiddled his razor and said, 'None, Pilot.'

This was Costra's affectionate nickname for him on good days. He seemed relaxed and happy. The scar on his cheek was no more than a whitish furrow. Bernard was about to leave the cabin when his attention was drawn to a diamond ring, glittering in the ashtray.

Costa noticed.

'I shall raise about £15 from a Greek on that,' he joked, 'And then it's London for me.'

But the Corsican could not have had any illusions as to the difficulties which awaited him after his arrival in harbour. As soon as he set foot ashore, his usurped authority would be questioned. The whole edifice laboriously built up with persuasion and punches risked collapsing. In a few hours his team might scatter. Fortunately, as Costa knew, the British forbade foreigners landing before they had been subjected to a certain check-up. It was during this period that he would have to make sure of the *Le Rhône*. It was therefore important for him to clear up the essential points immediately.

General de Gaulle had obtained recognition as head of the Free French as from the 28th June. This action on the part of the British Government theoretically placed the *Le Rhône* and her crew at the disposal of the London Committee. Costa insisted that he would not abide by this decision. There was no proof that the authorities would leave him in command of a ship he had taken over merely for the Las Palmas affair. Moreover, in all probability the old 'tramp' would probably be given some menial task. Having frequented the Colonial administration and haunted ministerial antechambers, maintaining that he was a nephew of Albert Sarraut, the Corsican distrusted 'the croakings of armchair sailors.' Moreover, a certain number of elementary questions might be asked to which he did not wish to reply.

On the British side there were plenty of obstacles, but the *Le Rhône* now possessed a trump card which had been won after a tough struggle in Gibraltar – the Blue Ensign. Thanks to the flag flying at her masthead, the old tub which was about to enter Barry Docks was a British bottom. Exploiting a false situation, Costa could represent himself as the French captain of one of His Majesty's auxiliary ships. This, of course, would not stand up to close inspection. To begin with, the real captain of the ship was called Passementton and the old briefing which gave Costa the prerogatives of captain did nothing to alter the fact. Next, it was not sufficient to fly a new flag to change your nationality, and finally, the officers and crew remained divided. Even though some of them envisaged continuing the struggle under Costa's orders, others dreamed of joining their respective battalions or of returning to France. In spite of all these difficulties, the master of the *Le Rhône* had resolved to offer the Admiralty a coherent unit – a ship, a crew and a captain. He confessed as much to Soigne. It was of little matter that the boat was ancient, the crew unreliable and that the command had been usurped. The ensemble alone counted.

Of what service could the *Le Rhône* be? Costa had given this some thought. He wanted to turn her into a commerce raider. The title pleased him and he anticipated the savour of the fruitful and bloody consequences. One expression kept recurring in his adventurous declarations: 'I shall demand a privateering commission from the King of England.' Alas, the International Declaration of Paris in 1886 stipulated 'Privateering has been and will remain abolished.'

Moreover, the term 'a privateering commission' which delighted Costa was inaccurate. He should have said 'Letters of Marque.'

'His Majesty gives leave, power and permission to Sir Costa, Claude-André, to arm and equip for war a ship named *Le Rhône* of 2,450 tons, with a certain number of men, cannon, powder, lead and other munitions of war and the provisions necessary for him to sail in a state of seaworthiness and to harass the Corsair pirates and vagrants obeying the orders of Chancellor Hitler.'

Costa knew perfectly well that times had changed and that such a commission could no longer be delivered to him, but accustomed to border-line action, to permanent illegality, he hoped to find some compromise, if not with Heaven, at least with the Admiralty. In the 1914–18 War the German Lückner had been dubbed the 'Last Corsair,' and in the Allied camp Commander Campbell with his Q-ship had sunk a great number of enemy submarines. A place might be found for the *Le Rhône* in this form of unorthodox warfare which called for singular temerity. Anything was better, at all events, than submitting purely and simply to the laws of the Merchant Navy.

Costa did not impart his intentions to the crew. Soigne alone had elaborated a few of the lieutenant's remarks and tried to form some lucid picture from them. No one could fail to see that above all Costa wanted to fight, but the doctor was intent upon discovering other motives beneath this obvious patriotism. Money? The new skipper of the *Le Rhône* probably did not despise it, but it certainly did not dictate his behaviour.

'War is not for choirboys,' he once said in the mess during one of his rare appearances. 'Whoever is ready to die well has a perfect right to live well.'

With an authoritarian fist he had subdued the captain and crew of a merchant ship and brought them to England. The British paid a heavy premium to any fighting man who delivered them an aeroplane, a crew or a ship. The Corsican had right of capture if his command of the *Le Rhône* was recognized from the precise moment when, with the aid of Patte, he had slipped away from the convoy in the Mediterranean. From that date, according to the code of privateering, the ship had been 'an object of forfeiture entitled to prize money.' The premium, according to the traditions of the sea, had to be shared between the captain and the crew.

The behaviour of Costa at the moment of sharing the prize would show how disinterested he was.

No, money was not the secret spring which made the lieutenant's mechanism function.

Soigne thought of a desire for honours. Costa did not despise tradition and behaved on board ship like a captain who has raised a crew and paid it at his own expense. Official receptions, such as the one given to Admiral Muselier in Gibraltar, did not displease him. Moreover, he had confessed to two ambitions – to be a commander in the Royal Navy and to win the DSO.

But neither did this explanation suffice. Costa must have a collector's passion for stripes and medals, such as he displayed in the panoplies of weapons on the walls of his cabin. Weapons! Perhaps that was the key to the puzzle – the key to the man.

Even more than patriotism, fighting for fighting's sake was probably Costa's greatest ambition.

Soigne observed his chief when he told him that the *Le Rhône* was entering Barry harbour. He saw the lieutenant button his cuffs, do up his jacket and, before leaving the cabin, see that the ring was in his pocket.

CHAPTER FIVE

ASSIGNMENT LAS PALMAS

From Passementton on the bridge to the ship's boy who had been recruited at Gibraltar and had finally got over his sea-sickness, the crew watched the tangle of the docks emerge. It was a complicated world – a network of rails glittering in the sun like fugitive snakes, a forest of masts, gasometers and oil tanks above which floated a layer of smoke. The war had set its seal of monotony on everything; no trace of gleaming brass. The British warships lined up as though on parade, grey and lifeless, seemed like bars of lead.

As they coasted along the shore the sea became civilized and at the same time filthy. Already the first floating logs, iridescent patches of oil and industrial odours began to circulate around the old cargo boat.

'We are getting near land!' shouted Bernard. 'It already smells of mussels.'

The *Le Rhône* passed a dry dock. A ship inside, solidly shored, had patches of red lead on its hull, like bleeding wounds. A host of workmen were busy on its sides and the blue flames of their oxy-acetylene lamps could be seen.

They entered the inner harbour through a narrow bottleneck. Led by the tug, the *Le Rhône* veered slightly to port and came alongside opposite a fleet of tankers. As soon as the gangway had touched the ground some British officers came aboard. Their leader asked to speak to Lieutenant Costa.

Lolling against the wall of his cabin with a cigarette in his mouth, Costa appeared calm.

'Johns,' he cried. 'Whoever would have thought this six months ago in Paris.'

The smooth, red-faced Englishman reeked of Virginian tobacco and good living. At the mention of Paris he shrugged his shoulders and gave the ghost of a smile.

Madeleine Guesclin did not utter a word. With lowered head she seemed to have taken refuge in a hostile reserve. Offering her his cigarette case, Johns asked: 'What about the explosive?'

'Oh, it's quite safe,' she replied with a nervous laugh, 'I'm sleeping on it.'

The Englishman could not help giving a start.

'You've kept it in your cabin?'

'Yes, under my bunk.'

Costa chewed as though playing with the bullet which had once torn his cheek.

'Guesclin is a funny girl,' he said. 'She'd rather have "Plastic"* in her bed than a man.'

At the word 'plastic' Johns automatically looked round at the door before continuing with the girl.

'But it's highly dangerous. The least jolt could have set off the detonators.'

Guesclin crossed her legs and pulled down her skirts.

'Oh, I'm not crazy. I put the detonators in cotton wool and gave them to the gunnery officer.'

'And where did he put them?'

'In the drawer with his shirts, under his bunk.'

'That explosive must be sent without delay to London,' said the Englishman after a short silence.

Costa broke in: 'That's just what I intend to do, old man, but one good turn deserves another. I need you. I took this boat by force, and now my position has to be established.'

---

* It must be remembered that in 1940 'Plastic' still was unknown to the Germans. Without Costa and Guesclin, the secret of this explosive would have fallen into the hands of the enemy on his entry into Paris. The British therefore owed a great deal to Costa.

Half an hour later, glass in hand, Costa was addressing his officers in the mess room.

'Gentlemen, the moment for joining Great Britain in this war has at last arrived. The full complement of the *Le Rhône* has been accepted by the Royal Navy. Each officer will shortly receive a commission and we shall continue the fight under the White Ensign.'

There was great applause and glasses were raised. The impassive British visitors gave an approving smile.

'During the short lapse of time between your admission into the Royal Navy and your papers being in order,' Costa went on, 'you will all have to remain on board. Our Allies have asked us to observe the same strict discipline which is in force among themselves. On the night of the 24/25th August the first German bombs fell in the centre of London. On the following day the RAF bombed Berlin. Total war is now to be waged. Everyone in Great Britain is convinced that the Boche are preparing an invasion. It will be repulsed. But each ship which seeks refuge in a British port can harbour a spy in the pay of the Nazis. The security regulations are categorical – everyone is confined to the ship.' The same evening Costa left with Johns for London.

He returned three days later. A temporary office was installed opposite the engineers' mess for Johns, Commander Harley, OC Barry harbour, and Costa. One by one the officers of the *Le Rhône* were asked to step in. When Passementton was asked to adopt an English patronymic, he hesitated.

'Is that really necessary?'

Since Gibraltar he had been like a ship which has broken adrift. Nothing was being done in accordance with the regulations and now he was being asked to sever an essential tie – his surname. At that moment he must have seen himself standing before the directors of the company in their office in the Boulevard des Dames.

'Captain Passementton, what have you done with your ship?'

He could hear the traffic on La Joliette and the hooting of the ships' sirens as they left the harbour. Familiar odours and noises beckoned him.

'But why do you want me to change my name?'

Costa burst out laughing.

'I don't know if you're aware of it, Uncle, but you've already been condemned to death. Vichy has issued a decree applicable to all those who did not comply with the armistice. In London they are arranging to give 'a ball for those condemned to death' – you'll be perfectly entitled to go.'

More consoling and with a trace of embarrassment in his voice, Johns confirmed the necessity.

'Captain, I fully understand your scruples, but if by some unlucky chance you were taken prisoner . . .'

The old man breathed deeply. He fiddled with the leather wallet in which he kept his papers.

'Come on, Uncle,' said Costa, without sparing him, 'what about calling yourself Shakespeare?'

Passementton thought and at last found a name which in the circumstances was extremely pathetic. In order not to break completely with the past he adopted the affectionate name used by his wife and himself in their letters: '*ton Doudet . . . mon Doudet.*' 'Doudet,' he said clumsily. Pen in hand, the British petty officer repeated.

'Ow! Dowdett.'

On the verge of tears, the captain of the *Le Rhône* spelt out D-o-u-d-e-t as though burning his tender missives one by one. Nevertheless, before he left, he turned to Costa and asked:

'And what name have you chosen?'

'Me? Langlais, obviously.'

In a dark blue skirt and roll-necked sweater, Madeleine Guesclin sat at a table. With hardly a trace of make-up and her hair allowed to go free, she was showing her legs.

'And Guesclin?' asked Costa. 'Do you know what her name is now? Barclay. That's handy. By transposing the syllables it becomes Clébard, a mongrel bitch!'

When it came to Soigne's turn he chose O'Leary; Bernard hesitated for a moment and Langlais baptised him Archibald. The other Belgian, Brinchant, became Peter O'Neill. Grillo, the ex-naval officer, Fontenay; Patte, the engineer, Rogers; Rinto, the gunner's mate, Lagrange; the third engineer, Patterson ... The ratings became Pearson, Patrick, Powell, Marsh, Brown ... a few of them had suggested Nelson, Marlborough or Hudson Lowe, but each time a courteous refusal on the part of the British nipped any such jest in the bud. When they came to the Arab stokers from Djibouti, they were found to possess two out-of-date passports, one French, one British.

'Well, I'm blessed, they thought of it before we did,' remarked Costa.

The list was finally complete. It made Langlais captain of the ship with Doudet and O'Leary as his seconds in command. All the passengers of the *Le Rhône* were given a rank superior to that which they should by rights have held. Archibald and O'Neill were promoted lieutenants, as was Fontenay, who, expecting to be treated better than O'Leary, could scarcely conceal his annoyance. Barclay became a Wren officer, the only woman in Great Britain to hold a commission in a warship.

Nevertheless the former captain was still not satisfied.

'That's not all,' he said when the formalities had been completed. 'What are we going to call the ship?'

After forcing the nationality of the *Le Rhône*, playing havoc with the officers' hierarchy, forcing his men to change their names, having on all counts appeared completely unfaithful to the letter to be faithful to the spirit, Costa invented his final paradox: 'We'll call her *HMS Fidelity*', he announced.

While waiting for their official acceptance into the Royal Navy, the Frenchmen and Belgians were allowed to go ashore. Barry Docks, where the ship was tied up, was a town on its own from which they could not leave without showing a pass to the Special Police. The whole industrial and maritime area was confined on the ground by barriers and in the sky by barrage balloons. The harbour precincts had been raided for the first time on the 15th July at 10 o'clock in the morning, without causing much damage; two weeks later the Luftwaffe had dropped a bomb on a farm in the open country.

Barry possessed the usual defences against air attack – ack-ack batteries, smoke screens, barrage balloons and huge reserves of water to fight eventual fires. At nightfall the city was fully blacked out with the exception of the port workshops and the yards, where work continued. This limited black-out added an additional frontier between the quays and the rest of the lo-cality. In case of a raid, a single switch could plunge Barry Docks into total darkness.

Thompson Street – the main street – and the Barry Docks Hotel were the haunts of a nondescript crowd, the variegated fauna of a harbour where negroes, Asiatics, Europeans, refugees and British sailors rubbed shoulders. On the 5th September, Langlais took O'Leary to a small dance hall which reeked of Virginian tobacco and beer. The air could have been cut with a knife and the guests were obviously slightly the worse for drink.

'I can smell a brawl,' said Langlais, sniffing the air greedily.

Nevertheless, he did not look for a scrap, as O'Leary had feared. He confined himself to staring insolently at the tarts, most of whom were in uniform, dancing check to cheek with sailors. He kept muttering between his teeth. 'They're hideous enough to make Barnacle Bill himself turn queer.'

Having got this off his chest, he sat down in front of a bottle of gin which he had brought from the ship, ordered glasses and seemed completely disinterested in everything. Suddenly he looked his companion straight in the eyes:

'Mortiss, you must be wondering if I take you for a nitwit. Now that you're my second in command you have a right to some explanations. There's no need for you to know everything and I've no intention of telling you nothing but the truth. As long as I produce a Costa you can accept and who suits myself, we should both be satisfied. The others will never get as much. As to real confidences, that's all right for women – you're worth more than that. How old do you think I am?'

'Between forty and forty-five.'

'I was forty on 7th April last. I was born in Hanoï and completed my studies at the merchant navy school at Marseilles. I passed out as a wireless officer. Is that OK with you?'

'Why not?' replied O'Leary, with a smile.

'On my return from Indo-China I became a spy for the Colonial Ministry. Well, hold your horses. First mission – Paris-Bangkok in an ancient jalopy on the pretext of scientific research. Officially, I worked for the Musée de l'Homme, but on the side for the Cinquième Bureau. I went to Berlin and on the rifle range of the St. Hubert Club I made rings round Papa Goering ... From there I went to India and Siam where I wandered through the country disguised as a Bonze with my begging bowl and a revolver within reach. I brought back photos of flora and fauna for the Museum and information for the Service about the Japanese preparations. I was paid for both on my return to Indo-China. There I met Guesclin. She had been living in poverty since her husband was assassinated in Somaliland by the Italians. I put her on her feet again and consoled her. It was all the more merit to me because I had a son of my own on my hands.'

O'Leary raised his eyes as though this event intrigued him far more than the picaresque adventures which went before. Langlais tried not to notice his surprise and went on:

'Yes, a son of my own, whom I wanted to make a man of. If

we ever get out of this war alive we shall do great things together,' he announced.

Langlais brought a photograph of a baby from his wallet and handed it to Soigne. 'Here, take a look at this. Do you think he's a success? I had the mother chosen by a quack.'

It could have been any little three- or four-year-old Eurasian. The Belgian was reminded of a poster advertising a certain Indo-China noodle. Langlais was radiant. He put the picture back in his pocket with the pride of a head clerk who has just shown his 'latest' to his assistant.

'And don't say you think he's a hideous little brat, or I shall demote you.'

The skipper's paternal feelings seemed to suggest that he would betray more confidences. O'Leary tried to take advantage of this.

'And what are we going to do now?' he asked.

'I'm going to surprise you, *mon vieux*. We nearly landed up in French Equatorial. Muselier thought we should arrive in England before the 26th August and was counting on us for a raid which is being planned on Dakar* ... Unfortunately we arrived too late, and we shan't be in the show.'

He was smoking and seemed lost in thought.

'What bloody awful music,' he said softly, as though the din around him prevented any escape. Then he turned to his second in command: 'Mortiss ... remember what I tell you now. We're going to do great things together. There's only one real war every twenty-five years, and we're lucky enough to be the right age for it. Yes, we're going to have a crack. The British can't refuse me anything. I brought them back a package which they wanted like hell. Twenty-five pounds of explosive which the Boche would have given a great deal to get their hands on. It was all I had left after Las Palmas.'

---

* The *Le Rhône* had actually been detailed for Operation Menace which took place off Dakar between the 23rd and 25th September, 1940.

'What happened at Las Palmas?'

O'Leary's question was spontaneous. It had been in his head for so long that it sprang naturally to his lips. For once Langlais did not avoid the issue. He looked up at a fair-haired giant in British battle dress who had bumped into him by accident, and apologized with a smile. Then he returned to the conversation.

'In November 1939, seventeen German cargo ships, representing a total of 73,000 tons, were blocked in the Canaries. The choice fell on the *Corrientes*, which had left Hamburg on the 14th August – a fortnight before the declaration of war – and which was waiting at Las Palmas to be able to proceed to Santa Fé. We had to blow it up discreetly, without causing any complications with the Spaniards. It was at this moment that I received my briefing to come aboard the *Le Rhône*. You should have seen Passementton's face the morning I shoved the paper under his nose . . . and the following day, when I brought Clébard aboard. At the end of April we were on the spot after putting in at Agadir. The gay life . . . grub in the best hotels, peacetime what? I used to drink with the German officers and maintain that "sailors have only one country – the sea." We were invited on board. To keep my hand in I relieved them of most of their pay at poker. We got on magnificently. One of them was kind enough to show me on the map of the harbour stuck up in the hall the exact position of the *Corrientes*.

'But now we had to work out the coup. During the crossing I came to an arrangement with that swine Marais and with Patte . . . They were all for it. On the evening of 8th May the *Le Rhône* put to sea and left territorial waters. On the night of the 9th/10th we put about and made for the harbour with our lights extinguished. I gave orders for the launch to be lowered and embarked with Marais. The limpet mines were handed down to us. They were red half-globes filled with "Plastic", with a magnetic plate to attach them to the hull. The boys handled them as they would have handled Mae West's bra. I had told them that the slightest clumsiness on their part and we should all be blown to kingdom come. We took our bearings on the Las Palmas beacons to reach the outer harbour where the *Corrientes* was moored. As soon as we sighted the ship we dropped over the side . . . a midnight bathe. Pushing our mines before us we swam towards the cargo vessel. "You can't miss a mass of 4,565 tons," Marais kept saying: "So the prize money's settled, eh? Fifty/fifty?"

'The *Corrientes* was surrounded by lighters filled to the wales with coal. I slipped between them. Everyone must have been asleep on board. You can imagine it – a neutral port and in May. I swam under water, coming up occasionally for air. When I got to the hull, I attached the limpet mines below the water line. Marais did the same. We pressed on the pencil detonators, set to explode two hours later. Mission accomplished. We swam back to the launch, climbed aboard the *Le Rhône* and left for Marseilles. We arrived just in time to enjoy the Italian bombardment and to see the cargo vessel *Chellah* peppered in front of our eyes. At last we tied up at La Joliette and Uncle could go ashore and drink his *pastis* in peace.'

Three hours later the wail of the sirens rent the night. Archibald, who was one of the first on deck, saw Langlais appear; he was struggling into his clothes to have a look at the sight.

'Ah, some action at last!' . . .

The siren wailed like a banshee. All the lights in the harbour had gone out as though by magic. The dark sky seemed to be a vast shell which amplified the wailing. Langlais came up to Archibald who was leaning over the rail looking up at the sky.

'Look! Pilot, how calm it all seems when the lights go out.

On an evening like this we shall take the *Fidelity* into Kiel harbour and blow everything up.'

Even before the throb of the planes' engines could be heard, the first bombs fell on Barry.

CHAPTER SIX

EMERGENCY WARRANT

On board the men were awaiting for their papers to come through. Without news from their occupied countries the crew of the *Fidelity* tried by every means – still numerous and complicated at this period – to correspond even in a sibylline manner with their families. They used *postes restantes* in Switzerland, Portugal or Spain. Doudet wrote long screeds to his wife.

'He must be telling her that he's winning the war singlehanded,' Langlais said maliciously.

On Saturdays the officers went to Cold Knapp, the headland west of Barry, where they found a swimming pool, rows of bathing huts, white cottages, well-tended lawns and a lake for canoeing. Had there not been so many uniforms, it might have been peacetime. Perambulators, nurses, balloons, bicycles, icecream vendors ... Every Englishman too old to fight had volunteered either as Air-raid Wardens or Home Guards and the older women served as nurses and with the Red Cross. The Blitz was the great topic of conversation. Everyone discussed the exact number of Huns shot down on that famous 15th September. The BBC announced that 185 enemy aircraft had been brought down, although the Germans only admitted to 56 missing. Another subject was the losses from U-boats in the Atlantic, which sometimes reached fifty ships a month, and finally, there was great conjecture as to what America would do.

At Bindles, the smart club at Cold Knapp, the French met their compatriots, the aviators from the St Athan airfield five miles away. Together they recalled far-off France and were furious at being here inactive when the war was raging elsewhere. The sailors of the *Fidelity* felt very superior to the pilots who were condemned to fly their link trainers and to take technical courses on the ground. Confident in Langlais, they expected to be in action in a few days, without having to go through the depressing official channels. They realized that they were waging a war of their own.

However, at nightfall, as they returned to their ship along Whitmore Bay, the sailors felt homesick. Everything was too calm, too British. The road was flanked on one side with hotels and the seafront shops; on the other side a park with flower beds, the covered promenades of the beach and the long stretch of sand when the tide was out. They only had to stop and lean on the balustrade, to look at the sea, to be filled with emotion. Beyond the Bristol Channel was only another strip of Britain, like this, usually hidden in the mist. But one could ignore it and submit to the childish spell of the 'other side of the ocean.' Far away, beyond another channel to the South, beyond the green of the shallows and the hazy horizon where sea and sky mingled, was France, familiar in the old days, now mysterious and hostile.

By turning away they were back once more to a strip of tarred road, the smell of petrol, ice-cream advertisements, refreshment bars, the neon lights of the Roxy, the coats of arms on the stratoglobe in the Amusement Park, closed during the war. Imitation rocks covered with snow, chaotic mountain peaks joined by miniature viaduct, big wheels and the arena made the place look like an abandoned fair. In the centre of Barry Island rose the white arches of the railway station.

This frustration gnawed at their morale which was already low as a result of inaction. Now that their first advance pay had been spent in dance embraces and heavy drinking bouts, the men felt physically relieved, restless in spirit. In its wake came a need for tenderness. One by one the officers fell in love with

English girls, from some family which had welcomed them.

Langlais smiled at these budding idylls.

'If we're here a few more months I shall have to install a crèche.'

Archibald screwed up his eyes and a smile appeared at the corner of his lips. He began to philosophize on this forced inaction.

'Ever since we came aboard this "tub" we've been waiting. We had to wait to leave Gibraltar, then to get to Barry, and again for our commissions. When we've got them in our pockets, we shall wait before we leave Barry. Wait after wait, and the armistice will soon be signed. On that day, they'll make us wait before we march down the Champs Elysées.'

One morning a row of trucks pulled up alongside the *Fidelity*. In the pouring rain the sailors received orders to open the hatches, man the derricks, and unload the merchandise they had taken on at Marseilles. Everything was unloaded with the exception of the wine and spirits, which Langlais declared unassignable – bales of cloth, bicycles, cases of sugar and boxes of trash.

In his short sou'wester, Doudet attended the authorized pillage of his ship and insisted upon an official discharge note for his company.

'What company?' asked Langlais. 'The *Le Rhône* no longer exists and the *Fidelity* is one of His Majesty's ships.'

Blaise took possession of the necessary stock to maintain the culinary traditions on board. Each man received an issue of linen and sundry necessary articles. O'Leary looked on impassively. Sheltering beneath a truck, he checked the chests before they were loaded on to the agent's trucks. He only relinquished his post to Archibald when one of the sailors cut his hand badly on an iron hoop.

'Go on with the tally. I'll look after this clumsy lout.'

By tea-time the *Fidelity*'s holds were empty. The rain continued to beat down on the plates and the breeze made the awnings flap like damp cloths.

The following day Langlais took the train to London. He was in high spirits when he returned three days later. At cocktail time he showed the officers the *Fidelity*'s coat of arms which he had had drawn by a man from the College of Heralds. It bore the proud device: *Honneurs ne cherche, fidèle je suis.*

'*Honneurs* with an "s",' he insisted. 'And that's not all. I've great news for you. Our ship has just subscribed for two Spitfires which will participate in the battle for Britain under the names of *Fidelity I* and *Fidelity II*. That is a tribute we owed to our British Ally.'

Armed with his empty ship, a letter of thanks from the RAF, and his past prowess, Langlais could now negotiate with the Admiralty. Nevertheless he still had to outwit the Free French who had cast their eye on the *Fidelity*. He embarked upon conversations with them, alternatively friendly or excitable, but always sufficiently vague to have something in reserve. From one week to the next he changed abruptly from courtesy to threats. One day he would receive a Gaullist on board with the greatest pomp and on the following day, when a dozen French officers asked to visit the ship, he posted sailors with tommy guns on either side of the gangway and only let them come aboard in pairs. Any means served to disconcert and to gain time.

After the visit of an almoner from the Free French Forces who complained at not seeing men from the *Fidelity* at Mass, he ordered the crew to attend in relays each Sunday. A week later he gave the same satisfaction to an Anglican parson. Before his officers he did not disguise his feelings and maintained that three-quarters of the Free French worked in the BBC.

'France has become a nation of broadcasters.'

Changing thus from hostility to understanding, Langlais ensured the momentary neutrality of the Free French while he embarked upon his real struggle with the Secret Service and the Royal Navy.

Sponsored by Johns – with whom he had a bond from the Las Palmas and the plastic affairs – the Captain widened his official contacts and finally met the 'little fellow' – this was the nickname of Smith, the Grey Eminence of the entire Naval Warfare. On the other hand, Barclay – soon to be first officer of the WRNS, came out of her apparent apathy and renounced her sunbathing. Dressed in a very severe coat and skirt cut by some modest yet honest British tradesman, she set about obtaining the protection of the Marquise de C., one of the heads of her service.

O'Leary was the first to know the results of these underground dealings and society recommendations. Langlais had succeeded in being regarded not only as the sole captain of the *Fidelity* but also as its legitimate owner. Instead of taking a substantial outright payment, he chartered his boat 'to make war' in return for a profitable monthly payment from his British partners. Flying the White Ensign, the old *Le Rhône* was indissolubly bound up with Langlais and when the latter set foot on deck he could assess the whole extent of his new power. No one would ever take his property away from him.

The *Fidelity* was built in 1920 and could not become a fighting unit without undergoing a considerable transformation in the Liverpool naval dockyard.

The sailing date was fixed for the last days in December. Christmas was spent on board ship. Since the regular commissions had not yet arrived from London, Langlais decided to go and demand them in person. On the 25th, in the absence of the captain, the officers served the men with breakfast according to the best traditions of the British Navy.

When Langlais returned from London he announced that the nominations would not be long delayed and brought his fellow officers greetings from Comdr. Brown whom he had run into in the corridors of the Admiralty. After being laid up for three months, the *Fidelity*'s boilers were lit and she prepared to leave the Bristol Channel by night.

The ship dropped anchor a few miles from Barry with engines stopped to wait for daylight. She rocked heavily in the fog and groaned like a piece of wood about to split. Archibald, on duty watch, listened to the regular, disturbing cracks rising in the darkness. There was a sudden squall and the storm broke loose. Archibald decided to warn Uncle.

At that moment the cable broke. They could hear the anchor chain which had been violently released banging against the hull. With engines stopped the *Fidelity* began to list. Two men rushed to the winch to try and save the anchor but it had already been carried away. The vessel began to get way on and cries rose from all sides. 'Look out! We're drifting!'

'What's going on?'

In great haste the crew tried to release the second hawser but the ship had too much way on and everything was torn away – anchor, chain and winch. By some miracle neither of the ratings was injured. Unchained, lashed by the swell, the *Fidelity* plunged into the darkness like a mad dog; rolling wildly, huge icy waves swept the decks and the hull shivered as it received the resounding slaps. From the galley came the noise of broken crockery. Langlais had appeared half dressed as usual and was roaring his orders. But the fate of the ship was now entirely in the hands of Doudet. The old sailor had resumed control of the crew. With the tumultuous connivance of the sea, his leadership had been restored. He alone could extricate the ship from this peril. He roared down the speaking tube, simultaneously organizing the activities on deck and in the boiler room.

'Stoke up the boilers!'

It was a tough struggle. In spite of incessant changes of course, the *Fidelity* without driving power was heading for the rocks. An order to the helmsman and she set out again towards the other shore, like a ball rebounding from the walls of a corridor. On board, the sailors in a muck-sweat waited for the catastrophe. Langlais was foaming at the mouth. 'If the ship breaks up, I shall strangle the man responsible with my own hands.'

The ship had been fighting blindly for half an hour when someone cried: 'Good God, the Channel's mined!'

In the heat of the action this had been forgotten. Now everyone feared an explosion at the least error of judgment. Doudet continued to give orders from the bridge. He could feel his old companion of Mediterranean days groaning and shuddering under his feet. He saw her ship volumes of foaming water, twist beneath the onslaught of the waves; he felt like encouraging her as one pats a faithful animal. The good old *Le Rhône,* bewildered now that she had broken her cables, would only reply to her former skipper. All those who had made fun of the captain, irreverently calling him Uncle, looking the other way when they met him in the passages, were there, bowed by the storm, fingers stiff with cold, fear in their bellies, counting on him alone. Below, Fontenay acted with efficiency. Doudet heard his voice coming up the speaking tube from the engine room. He regained his sailor's respect for this ex-naval officer now busy trying to get the ship out of difficulties. Fontenay always used to say to Doudet's face, 'After the age of forty a merchant captain is either an incompetent or a drunken sot.'

And now fate had entrusted the salvage of the ship to these two men. In the face of their common danger, the sea, they discovered each other. In friendship their hands gripped the same helm.

At one moment the coast was so near that Langlais gave the order: 'Put on your lifebelts.'

But at last Fontenay managed to get the engines started. With corrections and counter orders the *Fidelity* managed to discipline her tacks and steer a course in the centre of the Channel far from the murderous minefield. A few moments later dawn broke. The crew stared at each other; weariness and terror had made their faces haggard. Doudet stumped down from the bridge, planted a cheroot between his wet lips and confined himself to saying before he lit it: 'Now there's nothing else to do but to return to Barry for repairs.'

Somewhat depressed after their misadventure, the *Fidelity*'s crew spent New Year's Day in Barry Docks, with the exception of a few officers, including Archibald, who went into Cardiff. It was freezing hard. The deck had been transformed into a skating rink; the rigging, taut beneath the ice, cut like razor blades, and rust had eaten into the guns and the winches. After their drenching in the Bristol Channel, everything they touched tasted of salt. They waited for a fall in the temperature to take the ship into dry dock at Barry where the Bailey Company was to carry out the modifications at the same time as the repairs.

Doudet digested his victory slowly as if it had been a good meal. Langlais seemed to have completely forgotten the incident. In the mess he recounted the details of his last night ashore spent with a little Scottish female soldier who knew everything there was to know about making love. Barclay listened to his confidences without a trace of emotion on her face. On New Year's Eve there was a heavy raid on Cardiff. Archie, stuck in the city with his fiancée, did not get back to the ship until two o'clock in the morning.

The days passed monotonously and everyone was thoroughly bored. Archie went skating on the lake at Cold Knapp. Langlais took rooms at the Hotel Gallia in town and appeared only occasionally, leaving all the responsibility of the ship to O'Leary.

Finally the long-awaited commission and warrant arrived. The *Fidelity* was chartered by the Admiralty dating from the 24th September, 1940, and posted to the Command of Western Approaches. The crew's enrolment dated from the 1st July, 1940, and they received three months arrears of pay. It was a triumphant moment. Rank, money, issue of uniforms arrived just in time to revive the spirit of a bunch of impatient youths whose ardour had been a trifle dampened by the incident in the Bristol Channel. O'Neill, nicknamed Pipite, was the first to receive a British uniform and to wear it proudly on board. Forced to pay a round of drinks, he had to submit to the jokes of Langlais who made fun of his small stature.

'It's not surprising that he got his first; they must have found it in the boys' department.'

Barclay soon appeared in her dark blue Wren's uniform with the three-cornered hat. Langlais, as soon as she appeared, said: 'Boys, ask her to show you her underclothes. You'll see, they're extraordinary.'

For once the girl rebelled.

'What do you know about it?'

He burst out laughing. 'Oh, it's quite simple. There's a camp in town just next to the gymnasium. You only have to climb on to the wall when the bugle blows at inspection time; they line up the girls and tell them to lift their skirts.'

Doudet, thoroughly shocked, choked over his glass.

Langlais tapped him amicably on the shoulder.

'Don't go getting any ideas, Uncle; their knickers come down to their calves. The airmen call it "blind flying".'

Now that they were in regulation uniform the men felt that they were really in the war. They complied with the traditional requirements that had so far been neglected – farewell letters to their families in case they disappeared and making their wills. Each left his belongings to his mate. Archie found himself heir to Rogers and a young cadet pilot officer of eighteen who had chosen Harrow as his alias after the school.

Those who embarked upon a serious love affair thought about getting married. Ferguson was the first to take the plunge, followed by Richardson, a man of forty-eight with a red face and a square chin. In civilian life his name was Leblond and he was a professor of literature. On board he was third engineer. One morning he found O'Leary busy compiling the routine orders for the day.

'I am going to get married,' announced Richardson.

'Congratulations, old man.'

'I wonder if you'd be my best man?'

'Of course.'

In spite of the comprehension his surprise received, Richardson did not seem at all at ease. He finally made up his mind and said, 'I think it's my duty to tell you that I've already got a wife in France.'

O'Leary could not repress a start.

'Well, my friend, and that doesn't worry you?'

'Me? Not in the least. I'd even like you to tell the skipper.'

Slightly bewildered, O'Leary went and saw Langlais in his cabin. He was greasing a long Herstal rifle which lay dismantled on his bunk.

'Take a look at this, Mortiss. I won the World Championship in 1937 with it. What brings you here?'

'It's like this. Richardson wants to marry a Welsh girl and he's already got a wife in France.'

'What the hell do you suppose that matters to me?'

Langlais looked down the barrel of his gun against the light.

'I've been married three times. You can tell Richardson I give him my blessing. But be careful – of Richardson, not of Leblond. On no account, not even for the purpose of getting married, must he give his real name.' The Corsican paused, and added: 'Particularly not at the Registry Office. In that way his mind will be at ease. As for Leblond, he was divorced by the Pétain regime. We have all been divorced from something or somebody, that's freedom, Mortiss.'

When O'Leary imparted the captain's instructions to the third engineer, he agreed.

'All right, I'll marry in the name of Richardson. In any case, my future father-in-law is a parson. He considers that a ceremony performed by a Catholic priest is invalid.'

A few weeks later Richardson was married in a small Welsh village. His witnesses were O'Leary and O'Neill, who were no more Irishmen than he was a real bigamist.

CHAPTER SEVEN

THE IRON RULE

Towards the middle of January *HMS Fidelity* with a full complement went into dry dock. The English stripped her old carcase, laying bare her rotten timber. The noises of hammers against the hull and the cries of the workers could be heard. Then an odour of tar invaded the cabins. Finally, when all the cracks were filled and the leaks caulked, the Bailey Company's workmen attacked the lower structure. They installed sleeping quarters on the spar deck, added several whalers to the two which already existed, erected a derrick to lower a heavy boat. The sailors who watched these transformations thought that the *Fidelity* was being refitted for landing operations.

Finally, when the carpenters erected huge mobile panels to modify the outer appearance of the vessel, some of the men changed their mind and thought she was to be a Q-ship. This had always been Langlais' expressed preference and apparently the Admiralty had adopted his idea. But the *Fidelity*'s transformation was still far from complete. One by one, two 100mm and a 25mm were installed in the bows and one 100mm and two 75mm in the stern. Then in the waist came two 25mm guns and sixteen 7·5 machine guns. At the sight of this arsenal Lagrange expressed his anxiety to Archibald.

'I don't like the look of it; they're going to use us as an ack-ack ship.'

The harbour authorities had probably thought of this, but Langlais had obviously destined the ship for adventures further afield. He left once more for London, accompanied by O'Leary.

Near Johns' headquarters, which was indistinguishable from an ordinary business premises on several floors, he left his companion and made a date with him at the Regent Palace Hotel, where he had booked rooms. Tired of waiting, O'Leary was walking up and down outside the hotel when his captain arrived like a whirlwind.

'Mortiss,' he said, 'we're off to have some fun.'

A new club had just opened in a cellar. Big red carpets ran down the stairs and below, under shaded lights, waiters in tails hovered round the tables. The room was full. The tabs on the uniform sleeves allowed soldiers of all nationalities who had flocked to London to be identified. Very much at ease in his British lieutenant-commander's uniform, Langlais demanded a seat next to the dance floor. He ordered a bottle of champagne and turning towards his companion said excitedly: 'If all goes well, we shall be in action in six weeks' time. But before that we've got to undergo intensive training. You'll have to form a commando group.'

The two conspirators were talking French and did not immediately notice a man in tails who came up to them.

'Excuse me,' he said to Langlais.

He had no time to finish his phrase.

'Who do you think you are, coming up without being introduced?' said the Corsican, furious at being disturbed.

'But I'm the owner of this restaurant,' said the man, slightly disconcerted, 'and I wanted to offer some champagne to my compatriots.'

'You're making a mistake,' said Langlais. 'I'm a Canadian.'

'Oh no, you're not, sir, you're French. I'm a Parisian and I ought to know.'

'Have you been in England long?'

'Well, since things were going badly in Paris I transferred my capital to London and . . .'

Langlais had pushed back his chair and turned to the man.

'And you joined up with a fighting unit at all speed?'

The man in tails was speechless.

'I pay for my own champagne,' said Langlais.

'Well, I must say, I think it's a bit thick . . .' The captain of the *Fidelity* had been waiting for this. In a flash he was on his feet. He seized the intruder by his butterfly tie and his lapels and lifted him off the ground. Indifferent to the protests from the dancers whom he jostled, he dragged his victim into the middle of the floor and with one blow sent him flying on the polished floor.

'That's what I do to rats of your type,' he said, returning to his table.

Three waiters had rushed up. Langlais turned round and O'Leary caught hold of the bottle by its neck. There was a moment's hesitation and cries of indignation. The waiters retired to rescue their boss who could not get up. An interpreter of the general disapproval, a Royal Navy commander started to give Langlais a rocket.

'Don't tire yourself,' said Langlais. 'I don't understand English.'

The redresser of wrongs continued to shout. The Frenchman gave him a thunderous look.

'If you want to join that puppet . . .' he said, pointing to the owner of the bar, who was taking refuge behind his staff.

The incident was closed, but Langlais insisted on remaining in the place until it closed.

At three o'clock in the morning the two officers were asleep in their room at the Regent Palace Hotel when the telephone rang in O'Leary's room.

'Get packed,' said Langlais, 'we're taking the 5.15 to Barry.'

'Anything wrong?' asked O'Leary, still half awake.

'No,' said his chief, roaring with laughter. 'Some brass hat reported our scandal in the bar. The Admiralty thinks that we're undesirable characters to be in London and has ordered us back to the ship at all possible speed. An order is an order.'

As soon as he returned aboard he assembled his officers.

'Gentlemen, in a few weeks we shall be putting to sea and we shall be in contact with the enemy. The whole crew is now to undergo intensive training in all branches. We are in British uniform in a British ship and in future I shall be giving my commands to British sailors.'

Each day a sergeant loaned by the Barry Garrison came to drill the men. Instruction was given in one of the hangars and the crew reported in relays. In addition to this military instruction which always began with intensive PT, the sailors were taught to shoot and to throw grenades. The training ground was on a hill outside the town and one afternoon Archie saw a clumsily thrown bomb ricochetting back down the slope. He had just time to shout and everyone flung himself on his belly before it exploded. This was the first time they had been under fire.

On Langlais' orders O'Neill went to the *Surcouf* which sailed in convoy between Great Britain and Canada. There he learnt his sailor's trade. Archibald attended the Gunnery School at Cardiff. Others went out on exercises in Royal Navy ships or on shoots in Barry harbour. Fontenay, after a course at the Royal Naval College, Greenwich, took over the role of instructor and gave courses in navigation. O'Leary was sent with Barclay on a sabotage course to a college somewhere in the North of London where commando officers and secret agents were trained. Rising at dawn, the men went for a run round the park, had to jump fully clothed into a pool of icy water and warm themselves up again later with a bout of unarmed combat. After breakfast the technical courses began – map reading, deciphering of codes, morse, dismantling of weapons, and the study of all types of explosives.

The 'Plastic' was contained in small beige-coloured cylinders five inches by one inch and rolled up in paper like modelling clay. These harmless little rolls became terrible weapons as soon as the detonator was introduced. A pencil containing a fuse attached by a wire was merely inserted into the plastic material. The wire itself was in contact with an ampoule of corrosive liquid. Under the pressure of a finger the glass broke and the wire began to erode. The yellow pencils caused an explosion in one, the blue in two, and the violet in twenty-four hours. Fuses that burnt a yard a minute, cigarettes with fulminate of mercury, TNT, detonators, bottles and incendiary lozenges which burst into flame spontaneously at a certain degree of moisture, coal briquettes stuffed with plastic, small gadgets designed for placing under motor car tanks, and limpet mines like those used at Las Palmas . . . Everything which could destroy boilers, vehicles, harvests, buildings or human beings was placed at the disposal of the saboteurs.

The afternoon was devoted to practice in the field. In turn the agents had to drive a locomotive, burn a house with phosphorus, throw a grenade, climb up a railway embankment and place a charge, modelled in advance to the dimensions of the chink, between the rails. Future emissaries of clandestine death, the men at this school made swift progress. They were made to crawl on their elbows with the faces in the mud, under live machine-gun fire. They were made to attack an instructor who was waiting for their onslaught with a bayonet. They went to bed at night with aching limbs and weary muscles, unable to forget these brawls.

Barclay passed all her tests with fantastic calm. The smell of powder or hand-to-hand fighting with an open blade made her eyes glitter almost as though with desire. Soaking wet like a dog as she came out of the pool, her overalls sticking to her body, she ignored her sex – to be more exact, she had none. Before breakfast she usually put on dry jeans and she got out of the others in front of O'Leary without a trace of shame. The water streamed from her shoulders and down her legs as she took off her trousers like a man. The Belgian, quite unmoved, waited for the moment when she would become a woman – but this never occurred.

What hideous hatred had produced this masculine will power? O'Leary thought of her husband who had been murdered by the Italians. But had she really been married? Did Langlais ever speak the truth? She never spoke about herself. Violent and free, she despised any exchange of confidences. And yet, there was a certain gentleness in some of her attitudes: she curled up in an armchair to read, exactly as a young girl would have done. But the novel she held in her hands was a manual of radio-telegraphy. Did she love Langlais? Did she love Love? Affecting a tone of banter, she spoke of embraces as of gymnastics and of immorality with a laboratory detachment.

Was she venial? She was undoubtedly very keen on money. Was this because she had suffered when she was starving in Indo-China? Cupidity may have become pathological in her case – a primeval instinct which dominated and perhaps stifled all the others.

Langlais gave her plenty of money but on the least excuse she would borrow a few pounds from some officer on board. She never repaid the loan. When the men had to make their wills, normally so distant, she went to great pains to get herself appointed as the beneficiary.

She was afraid of nothing and yet people felt a need to protect her. She was more courageous than an old soldier and no one had ever made a pass at her. Unapproachable, almost androgynous, she remained immured in her paradox, more securely than in any mystery.

Barclay was an expert with weapons. In the special cabin she perfected herself in rifle shooting. The room was plunged in total darkness and the agent waited with his finger on the trigger for a brief two-second illumination, enabling him to aim at the human silhouette which loomed up in one of the corners. The report had to occur before the target disappeared and the bullet had reached its goal, otherwise the one who fired was considered as dead. The young woman never missed her adversary. During the day she trained in front of a mirror to keep her hands fixed in relation to the wrist and forearm glued to the body, the enemy's navel presumed to be in the prolongation of the barrel.

Langlais came to the camp one morning unannounced to fetch his officers.

'Twenty days on this course are enough,' he said.

He took them to London for a night out.

He was staying once more at the Regent Palace and dined Chez Prunier. The whole evening he was in an expansive mood, jesting with O'Leary, telling the latest mishaps on board and asking Barclay if she had slept with the instructor.

'If you've done that, I shall challenge him to a duel,' he said. 'In any case it was on account of a duel that I had to leave the French Navy.'

The Belgian evinced no surprise. He accepted this new story with the same resignation as the others. After dinner, contrary to his usual habits, Langlais decided to return direct to the hotel. O'Leary thought he was in a hurry to be alone with Barclay and left the couple without having a nightcap at the bar. In the middle of the night a violent knocking on the door woke him up. Was this another of Langlais' escapades? No, it was Barclay in a nightdress with tousled hair, her face bathed in tears, asking for his help.

'He's in a mad rage,' she said to the Belgian, pushing the lock home in terror. 'He wants to kill me.'

She stood there, disconsolate and trembling. No trace remained of the proud commando Amazon.

'What's the matter with him?' she asked. 'He thinks I want to get some information from him about the coup he's planning. He's suspicious of his own shadow.'

O'Leary gave her his bed and slept on the couch, wondering what strange mission Langlais could have staged. When he awoke about eight o'clock Barclay had gone. He found her sitting with the captain at the breakfast table solidly tucking in to eggs and bacon. They both appeared in excellent fettle.

At Barry the repairs were well advanced. When it came to the interior refit, the officers had to leave their cabins and take a room in town at the Windsor or the Gallia or the Barry Docks Hotel. Langlais had given orders for a big bathroom to be fitted in his quarters and rented a villa in Cold Knapp with Barclay and Doudet. He often invited his junior officers who rode up the slope to Well Walk on commando's motobicycles. The cottage had a view over the gardens and the sea. Langlais liked to organize motorcycle races round the block, he always chose the best machine and pulled off noisy victories. Bobby, the Alsatian which Barclay had bought on her arrival in England, chased the competitors, barking loudly.

The beast's fidelity to the girl infuriated Langlais. When he made fun of her Bobby showed his fangs, raised his hackles and growled viciously.

One evening he could no longer control himself. He must have felt that Barclay took a delight in encouraging the animal's hostility. When the dog interfered again between them in the presence of the *Fidelity* staff at table, the Corsican flung himself on the beast. It was a jungle combat. Langlais tried to open the jaws which were savaging his forearm and concentrated on repelling the attacks of the now infuriated beast. Man and dog rolled together on the floor to an accompaniment of oaths and yaps of pain. Pale and tense, Barclay did not interfere. In her eyes it was a combat between two males and she let it continue. Langlais pushed over the chairs and thrust those aside who tried to intervene. 'Keep still you people, let me settle accounts with him on my own.'

It was a terrible scene. The quivering beast beat its paws in desperation against the walls. A rebellious leap and he bounded forward, insensible to blows, ready to die. The bloody, foam-flecked jaw banged against the sailor's fist.

'Vermin!' roared Langlais, 'he's torn off one of my nails.' They went into a savage clinch. The dog tried to bite and the man to seize the evasive muscular neck which trembled beneath his fingers. The last act took place under the table with a shuffling of feet like an embrace after a drinking bout. His sleeve in ribbons, and collar undone, his hands streaming with blood, sweating with pain and anger, Langlais staggered to his feet. Bobby had been tamed.

As the work gradually drew to a close the officers were able to re-occupy their cabins. They found them bare and smelling of oil paint. Since there was no training after sunset and Langlais showed himself liberal on this point, they frequently went ashore. It was usually a drinking party. It was a matter of honour to leave the ship with two bottles of gin – a boon to the civilians who were strictly rationed – to drink one during the evening with some casual pick-up and to make her a present of the second before leaving. These chivalrous traditions, according to Langlais, were part of the patrimony of the French Navy. O'Leary, when consulted in his capacity as a quack, was categorical.

'If alcohol did any harm, they wouldn't preserve things in bottles in the anatomy school. The main thing is to be reasonable and not to exceed a dose of a pint per man per day.'

The main problem was getting through the dock gates, but the men from the *Fidelity* were old hands. They went through whistling and usually returned in an advanced state of drunkenness, maintaining that the best place to conceal gin is in the stomach.

One night O'Leary was on watch on the bridge and neither Archibald nor O'Neill – on leave from the *Surcouf* – had returned for curfew. Feeling slightly anxious, the Belgian was pacing up and down the deck when he saw a shape loom up, streaming with water. Archie approached, very dignified, as wet as a strip of seaweed, his coat buttoned up to his chin and hat pulled down over his eyes. Walking like a robot, the lieutenant came on to the bridge followed by a hilarious and sober Pipite. Archibald saluted gravely and, leaving a long trail of sea water behind him, tried to reach his cabin.

'Where are you off to?' called O'Leary.

'To wash my uniform,' replied Archie, obviously trying to be civil.

'What happened to him?' O'Leary asked O'Neill who was trying to slip away unnoticed.

'Well, it was like this . . .' explained his accomplice, very considerately. 'We were walking along the quay and when we came to the canal bridge the lieutenant didn't see it.'

'He didn't see it?'

'No, positively not . . . or rather he must have seen it where it wasn't – and he fell in the water.'

O'Leary repressed an urge to laugh. Impassive, dripping like a sieve, Archibald politely agreed.

'Well, you see,' went on Pipite, 'there was a splash. I went down the ladder to help him up, but he insisted on climbing up alone.'

'Yes, alone,' echoed the sieve, with a shake of his head.

'On land once more he noticed that he had lost his cap, so he dived in again to fish it out.'

'A brand-new cap,' approved the sieve.

'Do you know what you're going to do, gentlemen?' said O'Leary.

It was obvious that they did not.

'You can be thankful that the skipper is at Well Walk and that you can use his bathroom. Archie must take a hot bath.'

'But I want to wash my uniform,' replied Archie, 'it's full of salt.'

'I couldn't care less. Take that bath at once, otherwise you'll catch pneumonia.'

The quack did not expect a quarter of an hour later to find Archibald fully clothed and cap on his head in a boiling bath, carefully sponging his coat.

'I'm getting the salt out of it,' he said with a smile.

Transformed from keel to truck the *Fidelity* returned to her berth in Barry Docks at the end of February. She was shortly to go on operations. Physically and morally the crew was ready. O'Leary had formed his commando team which included Barclay, Rogers, Ford, Ploëno, known as the 'Monster,' Ferguson and a dozen carefully chosen ratings. Having at last a renovated ship, powerfully armed and equipped with a crew which had acquired real military value, Langlais could look upon the future with optimism. A lot of water had flowed under the bridges in the last six months, since the day when, uncertain of his fate, Lt. Costa had waited for Johns at the top of the gangway of the ancient *Le Rhône*. With his brilliant promotion, which some considered rather scandalous, Langlais had entered the most exclusive world of all – the British wartime navy.

On his cabin door shone a copper plaque bearing the inscription, Comdr. Langlais, RN. His quarters consisted of a cabin with vases of flowers and his panoplics of weapons on the walls; a bedroom and bathroom which an admiral might have envied. On the other side of the corridor slept the captain whose vessel he had seized and, at the bottom of the companionway, Barclay, who had become a First Officer in the WRNS.

Langlais was now at the most delicate point of his climb – the point where, even in his own immediate circle he would be bitterly criticized.

Since the arrival of the *Le Rhône* in Barry, months had passed without the Gibraltar promises having been kept. Now assured of a comfortable pay, recognized as British sailors, the men of the *Fidelity* gave free rein to their critical faculties. The inaction weighed heavily on them and they felt that they had a right to some explanation.

'If only he'd tell us what he's going to do.'

O'Leary observed this rising discontent with anxiety. He was completely loyal to Langlais and was in no doubts as to his complete disinterestedness and patriotic fervour. He realized, however, that the skipper's behaviour displeased some people.

'He takes himself for Napoleon,' said Rogers the day Langlais came into the mess with a huge, lanky negro whom he had christened Daladier. Rings on his fingers, smoking expensive cigarettes from a gold case emblazoned with the arms of *HMS Fidelity* and sporting an ebony cane, Langlais never appeared without his Mameluke escort. He called the negro 'my son' and insisted upon irritating and rather grotesque marks of respect being accorded to him. It might almost have been said that he was doing his best to become detested.

Everything which might make him unpopular seemed to attract him. On board the chores multiplied; some were mere whims, exaggerations and often unjustifiable. His harassed crew began to grouse. O'Leary reported their mood.

'So they're not satisfied eh?' retorted Langlais. 'Well, I'll teach them how to obey.'

If the truth were to be told, the captain was as impatient as his men. He was homesick for France and in need of action.

Day after day the atmosphere deteriorated and the men continued to murmur. Old resentments which had been artifically extinguished blazed up like embers under the hot ashes. The names of Marais, Quesnoy and other sailors who had been victims of Langlais' brutality cropped-up in conversation. Finally, a small, particularly infuriated group sent a letter of protest to the Admiralty, claiming its share of the prize money which had not been received. Langlais seemed impervious. 'I'm keeping in touch with the gossip on board,' he replied curtly. Barclay tried to put him on his guard and was rudely rebuffed. O'Leary speculated on the reason for this sudden change of face. The cause of the trouble must be the negotiations between the captain, with the 'little fellow' as intermediary, and the Admiralty which were not going according to plan.

Rather than admit his difficulties to his brother officers, the Corsican apparently preferred to run the risk of alienating them. At a certain moment – when his British partners had given him satisfaction – he would know how to revive the enthusiasm of his men.

Langlais had adopted the same attitude towards his second-in-command. He never spoke to him except to give orders, O'Leary carried them out assiduously. He realized that the captain of the *Fidelity* and his crew were suffering from the same malady, from which only Doudet, always busy with his *pastis* and his mail, seemed exempt – an insidious malady which was slowly gnawing at them. They were all athirst for action. They had only joined with this goal in view. Coming from the four corners of France their association could only have some reason in battle. If they had followed Langlais, despite his outrageous behaviour, it was because in their eyes he was the incarnation of short term war.

Aboard the *Fidelity* they were merely men who had been drugged with heroism, who were being kept waiting for the ration of the drug.

'One good show, and everything will be all right,' thought O'Leary.

He could not know of course that the fate of all these men would actually be to run desperately after a combat in vain.

The captain had decided to keep up the combative spirit of his men at all costs. He purposely closed his eyes on the explosion of certain hotheads who organized nightly commando raids to ransack distant ships or trucks of material standing on one of the innumerable dockheads. The team set out in a truck at nightfall and pulled up before the chosen unit.

'Over there . . . the minelayer.'

One of the sailors got out, engaged the trusting sentry in

conversation, made him hopelessly drunk on gin or over-powered him before he could raise the alarm. From then onwards to hi-jack the small arms and reserves of spirits was child's play. In this way the *Fidelity* scrounged various access-ories, in particular a 20mm gun which was duly installed above the bridge. Young Harrow was furious at the unpleasant rumours current about their ship and its crew. Time after time complaints were sent to the harbour authorities and they ex-pected a search at any moment.

Archibald's marriage cleared the atmosphere which was be-coming almost unbearable. The lieutenant had gone to see Langlais a few weeks earlier.

'I want to get married, sir.'

'I'm not surprised.'

Archibald screwed up his eyes as usual and looked at his skipper.

'You're not surprised?'

'No – it was bound to happen if you kept going ashore.'

The ceremony took place on the 6th March at the girl's home. Harley, Langlais, Barclay and the other officers of the ship were present. The skipper gave the young couple a hand-some present with a card wishing them a pleasant honeymoon. 'See you soon, my pilot. See you soon, my girl. In better or worse times. My good wishes that you both come through all right.'

A few days later Langlais left for London. As he got into the little Cardiff train which passes under the Bristol Channel he confessed to O'Leary. 'This is the last jump. On my return we shall put to sea.'

The approaching departure encouraged O'Leary to give a little farewell party aboard. He invited some British officers and their wives, a few RAF pilots and the nurses from the Red Cross. Since Harley, harassed by the continual misdemeanours of the *Fidelity*'s crew, had for some days shown increasing sternness in service matters, Mortiss took his revenge by making his secretary drunk. The party, which was very gay, went on until 10.30. That is to say, it ended sufficiently early to allow the guests to get home before the 11 o'clock curfew.

At half past ten, alas, Harley's secretary was no longer capable of moving. Filled up with drink by O'Leary, she was lying like a sack of potatoes in an armchair. There was a brief confab with Fontenay.

'What on earth are we going to do with her?'

'Lock her up in one of the cabins.'

At midnight everyone retired to bed. At two o'clock in the morning the man on watch heard a deafening din coming from one of the passages. He ran to wake O'Leary who went and delivered his guest. The young girl was almost hysterical. She thought she was a prisoner and insisted on being taken home immediately.

'I want my mummy,' she kept screaming.

The Belgian hesitated. To reason with this fury was beyond his powers. On the other hand, to take her into town in the middle of the night would mean a stormy explanation with the dock gate police. At last he said: 'I'll get dressed. We'll take the truck and leave.'

At the prospect of being liberated the girl calmed down. She drank the coffee he had warmed and relapsed once more into a state of beatitude. The noise of the engine being started brought her back to reality.

'I want my mummy.'

She had to be helped down the gangway and hoisted on to a bench in the truck; a black duffle coat was thrown over her to hide her evening dress. O'Leary drove off. He cautiously avoided the patches of light beneath the blacked-out lamps and drove very slowly. But he had to stop at the gate.

'Make yourself as small as possible,' he whispered to his companion.

The man put his head through the left window after halting the driver of the French vehicle.

'Your pass.'

O'Leary handed it to him.

'You have no one aboard?'

'No one.'

Disbelieving, the sergeant walked round the truck and opened the other door. The deceit was unmasked.

'Your pass.'

The unfortunate girl burst into tears.

'I want my mummy . . .'

'Yes, we know all about that,' said O'Leary in a rage.

The MP, furious at being duped, insisted upon explanations. In despair the culprit handed him her identity card on which was inscribed 'Secretary to the Port Command of Barry.' The Englishman shrugged his shoulders. Immune to the girl's charms and O'Leary's amiable suggestions of a few bottles of gin, he made out a charge sheet. Only then did he allow the truck to leave. Thoroughly bored by this time, the Belgian dropped his guest at her front door, rang the bell and made himself scarce at the approach of mummy.

The following afternoon Langlais returned from London. The unusual calm aboard intrigued him.

'I suppose you've done something bloody stupid?' he said.

O'Leary decided to confess and told Langlais his adventure of the previous night in all its details. The captain could not believe it.

'Come, Mortiss. Tell me the truth. I suppose you had the girl?'

'No, sir.'

'You're not going to tell me that you took her home without doing anything?'

'Yes, sir.'

Langlais exploded.

'Do you realize that you've disgraced my ship?'

Seeing the argument take this trend, O'Leary breathed with

relief, but on the following day, his spirits sank. About eleven o'clock Langlais sent for him.

'I've just had an urgent call from Harley. You're coming with me.'

The air seemed charged with electricity. The Belgian wondered what sort of a storm there would be at this Franco-British meeting. Langlais was shown into Harley's office alone. O'Leary remained in the waiting room with the secretary. The girl said nothing. Blushing to the ears, she tapped away at her machine without raising her eyes. Through the door they could hear raised voices. Ten minutes later, Langlais rushed out and motioned to his second in command to follow him.

'Come along. Things aren't too hot. We'll talk about it on board.'

The two men swept down Thompson Street as though the devil was on their heels. The captain seemed nervous.

'The old man's in a hell of a stew,' he said. 'He wants to make a scandal. His wife must have given him a rollocking because he chooses girls who are too appetizing. He's going to send her before a court martial.'

Mortiss felt a prick of conscience. 'We must get her out of that.'

The captain of the *Fidelity* shrugged his shoulders.

'Oh, that's easy enough to say. If only you'd given her a baby we could have pretended that she was moonstruck. The English believe in those kind of stories. But no, you returned her intact. You've mortally offended them.'

Langlais must have been far more worried than he allowed it to appear. Since Gibraltar his relations with the British authorities had followed a carefully thought out plan. Realizing that there were great gaps in his script, he had chosen to be disconcerting so as to remain more enigmatic. Since his goal was to have his ship engaged he followed this policy towards the Admiralty and the highly intelligent 'little fellow' in order to attain his ends. He gave them spectacular occasions for reproach, but only minor ones which, without compromising the reputation of the *Fidelity*, kept him in the limelight.

This game demanded a skilful touch and he could not allow any outside interference. That is precisely what O'Leary had just done. By behaving like his chief, he had suddenly reminded the British of the danger that lay in contagion from the captain of the *Fidelity*. Barely tolerable on his own, Langlais became a positive menace when people began to ape him.

In his cabin O'Leary summed up the consequences of his previous night's escapade. The affair in itself was trivial. At most it merited a rocket from Harley. But by the way Langlais had reacted, he realized that the incident had embarrassed the captain. Doubtless the harbour authorities would veto a person who had become a little too importunate. What could be done? O'Leary shrugged his shoulders. After all, Langlais would know how to get out of this difficulty as he had got out of others, and he himself was ready to bear the brunt of his actions. He waited.

Towards midday the captain sent for him. The Belgian noticed the half-empty bottle of gin and the overflowing ashtray. Dressed in a shirt, Langlais opened the bathroom door. The water was still running down his legs from the shower.

'Mortiss,' he said, 'I think I've found the answer.'

He buttoned up his cuffs without being in the least embarrassed at wandering about like this half-naked.

'I'm sacking you.'

O'Leary believed him, for his tone was harsh enough.

'Not only shall I chuck you out but I'll have you court-martialled.'

The Belgian did not say a word. For the first time Langlais was behaving with the severity of a genuine ship's captain and he bowed to the decision.

'What can you expect?' the Corsican went on. 'I entrust my ship to you for three days and that's what you do with her.

Where do you think you are? Have you forgotten the respect you owe to your uniform?'

It seemed as though he would suffocate with rage. The scar on his cheek grew as hollow as a shell hole. Suddenly he burst out laughing.

'Admit you fell for it, Mortiss. Not a bad act, eh? It was the rehearsal of a little scene I propose to play tomorrow at a gala performance.'

An hour later Langlais sent an officer to Harley asking him to come aboard the *Fidelity* the following day at ten o'clock to discuss the serious affair in hand. The meeting took place in the wardroom. In his smart lieutenant-commander's uniform, a host of decorations on his chest, the captain of the *Fidelity* received the British officer and his assistant.

'Bring in Lt.-Cmdr. O'Leary,' he ordered.

The Belgian came in with the humble mien of a repentant sinner.

'So you have no sense of shame,' Langlais roared, catching hold of him by the tie. 'You behave like a drunken soldier. You transform a British warship into a brothel. Have you forgotten that you wear the uniform of a British officer?'

Under Langlais' heavy grip, O'Leary thought he would be strangled.

'You will be demoted and thrown out of the Navy, and you'll end your days in jail.'

The terrified assistant translated the invective to Harley.

The latter, red as a turkey cock, tried desperately to calm this human tornado.

'He hasn't deserved that.'

'Oh yes he has,' roared Langlais, without releasing his victim. 'I'm kicking him out of my ship. I never want to see his face again.'

'You're going too far.'

'Put him in irons,' roared the captain.

'Oh, come on, let him go.'

'I can't see why I shouldn't kill him.'

Harley suddenly assumed all his authority and mustered all his French to shout, loud enough to be heard: 'I insist that you pardon this man.'

Langlais let go of O'Leary as though he had been a sack of potatoes.

'Ah no, that would be too easy. This gentleman would strut about in a dishonoured uniform while a poor innocent girl paid the price for him.'

When the last sentence was translated, the Englishman probably realized that he had been hoodwinked, but it was too late. In any case, anything was preferable to a prolongation of this violent scene, so incompatible with the dignity of the wardroom in one of His Majesty's ships.

'The girl will not be charged,' announced Harley's assistant.

'Get to hell out of here,' Langlais shouted at O'Leary, who was only too pleased to leave the wardroom.

On the 11th March, *HMS Fidelity* left Barry for Liverpool. The great adventure had begun.

CHAPTER EIGHT

WATERS OF ANGER

The *Fidelity* spent a few days in Liverpool before receiving orders to join a convoy which was forming at Greenock.*

With the return of the fine weather and the approaching action, the morale of the crew was very high. Langlais had inaugurated the British rhythm of life on board. Each night at dinner the traditional toast was drunk. The captain served himself with port, passed the bottle from left to right and then, when everyone's glass was filled, announced: 'Mr Vice – the King.'

The 'Vice' was the youngest member of the wardroom present. He raised his glass and replied, 'Gentlemen, the King.'

The ritual took place seated. A wardroom in a British warship is the only place in His Majesty's realm where people do not rise for the King. This exception dates back to an unfortunate incident which occurred when a Prince of Wales invited aboard a cruiser on standing up to reply to the toast, forgetting how tall he was, banged his head on the ceiling.

Blaise served the meals in black trousers, white jacket and bow tie.

He was helped by Lagrange, the gunner's mate, and Cambon, the ex-aircraft mechanic. The brass shone and on the spotless white cloth there was a gleam of china and glass as in a luxury hotel. Throughout the day rum punch was at the disposal of the officers and the bar opened at 10.30. On the sideboard stood Suze, Pernod, gin and angostura. This gilded life

* *H.M.S. Fidelity* was in the convoy which was subjected to heavy U-boat attack described by Nicholas Monsarrat in his *The Cruel Sea*.

lasted for a week. Langlais seemed intent upon showing the British how he could lay on a feast. He received aboard with great ceremony and supervised the menu. The Corsair had become the lord of the manor. Everything conspired to enhance this welcome transformation. For a whole week there was no complaint against the crew and the *Fidelity's* British guests all left with the comforting impression that they had rubbed shoulders with sailors who were prepared for anything, but were highly respectable.

The preparations drew to a close. Water and coal had been taken on and the holds were full of vegetables, meat and butter; ice blocks for the provisions and the officers' mess had been delivered. A Breton ketch had been added to the existing small craft and the crew had not failed to notice the extraordinary quantity of various coloured paints stored in a special shed.

Where were they going? The ketch conjured up ideas of a raid on some French Atlantic harbour, but the mobile panels and the profusion of paint pots suggested a series of camouflages to deceive U-boats. Speculation was rife in the ship. Langlais' star was so much in the ascendant that his name was never mentioned. Harrow could nurse all his youthful honesty but his anxieties found no echo. Already lashed by storms on the open sea, dreaming of boarding and hand-to-hand fighting, swabbed down and polished from keel to crow's nest, the *Fidelity* prepared for battle with the blindness of an adulterous woman bathing herself to meet her lover.

At this juncture fifteen British Army officers arrived with their gear. Langlais gave orders for them to be put by twos and threes in the cabins available. They ate in the wardroom after the ship's officers had concluded the evening meal. There was no doubt about it; the hour of action was at hand. Who were these passengers whom the captain seemed anxious to prevent having any contact with the crew?

The convoy was scheduled to sail on Friday. Langlais demanded to leave Greenock on the previous evening.

'My ship will never sail on a Friday,' he insisted.

After an exchange of lively signals, the Admiralty bowed to this last capricious demand of the captain. The *Fidelity* left port alone, well ahead of the other vessels in the convoy.

As soon as she left the roads the engines were stopped and she waited for daylight to join the long file of ships zig-zagging towards the open sea. There were twenty-eight of them, escorted by small warships which had already begun to weave round them like sheepdogs. It was cold; the sky was grey and a fine drizzle was falling. The men had put on their sou'westers. When they met at their work they exchanged damp smiles of connivance. Joy could be seen written on every face. They were leaving!

The waves thundered against the hull. There was a tang of brine in the air and the old cargo boat came to life once more. She no longer shivered as before. The numerous transformations she had endured seemed to have infused new blood in her. The old 'tub' no longer sang as she had done in the old days; she leaped into the trough of the waves in a blaze of foam-flecked green. Water poured from every scupper. It spurted from her sides as from a watering can. Patte, who was not yet used to replying to the name of Rogers, had already analysed the odour of his ship.

'She smells British,' he declared.

The vessel's Triton-like joy was communicated to the crew. On deck there was all the activity of a building site. Despite the additional obstacles, consisting of panels, guns, small boats and all their gear – ropes, chains, Turks' heads, camouflaged awnings – the sailors threaded their way through surefootedly. His back to the rail, Archibald watched them at work. Only the passengers remained unmoved by the wave of happiness that spread through the ship. Wrapped in their waterproofs, always together, always mysterious, they smoked their pipes sheltered from the wind.

'They're speaking Spanish,' O'Neill reported as he returned from the stern.

'They're training,' replied O'Leary.

Archie wondered what the men were training for, but as usual he decided to wait for the facts before making his judgment. Nothing is more explicit than action.

Gradually they assumed the rhythm of the convoy. The changes of course imposed by the threat of U-boats made them tack like a group of turbulent children in a gymnasium. According to the humours of the sky and the route followed, the grey shadows of the allied ships increased or dwindled. At one moment only one was in sight, a moment later several. Occasionally the *Fidelity* seemed to be alone in the vast expanse of sea. All the other ships had been swallowed up in the distance or by the bad visibility. From time to time an escort vessel passed very close at full speed, throwing up a huge spray of foam.

The din of battle echoed off the Irish coast. Three Ju-88's appeared out of the thick cloud at low altitude. At first they were three dots, then their shapes grew more precise, brown and green, spotted with contrasting colours and illuminated by tracers. On all the ships, guns were blazing and the 'Chicago pianos' were in action. The sea was soon pock-marked as though someone had shaken a sieve over a bath. The sky was dotted with black and white woolly balls. Indifferent to the cross-fire converging on them, the three birds dived to wave level. They pulled out at the last moment to leap over a cargo vessel which they raked with short bursts or straddled with clusters of bombs. A few moments later they resumed their crazy course, skimming the surface of the water, spattered with spray.

Suddenly they dived on the *Fidelity*. The strap of his steel helmet cutting into his chin, Archie gave his firing orders. On the bridge, Langlais and Doudet watched the three attacking planes grow larger. In turn, the old cargo boat began to growl. As the guns fired she shuddered as through she had been stabbed. For the first time there was a smell of powder.

The aircraft seemed as though they would crash against the hull in their wave-top approach. Near the ship they seemed to blot out the whole sky. Three successive shadows crossed the deck with the boom of a tornado. Instinctively the men ducked. They heard the sharp crack of bullets on the plates and their exasperated whistle when they tore the wood of the rails . . . and the danger was past . . .

'A hit!' roared Archie.

He swivelled round on his firing seat as on a piano stool. Like a wounded gull, one of the Junkers had a plume of black smoke streaming from it. Its right wing seemed to dip into the spray. They followed its flight into the mist where it eventually crashed to its death.

There was a roar of joy from the ship and victory signs were exchanged in the hubbub. A sudden calm fell over the sea. In the distance there were a few dull rumbles of guns and then silence. At this moment the first cargo vessel sank. An invisible hand blotted it from the horizon. Laden with ore, it sank like a stone.

'U-boats!' roared Langlais.

The aerial ballet performed by the Junkers had been designed to distract attention while the U-boats grouped for the attack. Now they went into action. The white tracks of the torpedoes betrayed their presence everywhere. Harrassed and hard pressed, the convoy dispersed. One vessel was trying to escape its invisible attacker by flight: abruptly an explosion made her keel over and she sank in a seething whirlpool. Others vanished into the mist. In turn, the commodore's ship announced 'I'm sinking.' Tireless, the escort vessels waded into the attack, guided by the torpedo tracks. The *Fidelity* heard no more – neither the dull rumble of depth charges which seemed to rise from the depth of the sea nor the hideous sound of ships being hit. She was alone, lost.

Driven four miles off her course to the west, she continued her changes of course which would take her in a southerly direction. Night fell and it was bitterly cold. The men on board confined their remarks to their duties. It was not from fear; it was more a deliberate refusal to live in the present. They could only wait for the next moment. Perhaps a few hundred yards from the *Fidelity*, below the water, a U-boat was preparing to fire its 'tin-fish.' They did not want to know. Blind, deaf and obstinate, the ship continued to advance, taking comfort in the peaceful throb of its engines. And yet this very sound could denounce her to the enemy.

The sailors were not afraid. It was not the danger which forced them into silence but respect for the inevitable. Besides, they were waiting for nightfall. Soon they would slip into the cover of darkness. Nothing was more drab than this sunless twilight, this murky sky moist as a sick man's sheets. Suddenly Fontenay shouted: 'Over there! Look!'

It was difficult to see in the half-light. Were they pieces of wreckage? Drifting buoys? A cluster of flotsam? No, they were men's heads. The speed of the ship made them appear to be floating against the tide – half-emptied cockleshells carried away by a stream. No arms waving. Perhaps the unhappy men, numbed by the cold sea, were conserving their last strength in order to survive. Or perhaps the apparition had been too fugitive in the failing light to have distinguished their gestures of despair. In a flash everyone was on the port side. The implacable law of the convoy demanded that they should pursue their course; they could not stop, not even to lower a boat. Wherever there was a shipwreck there was a U-boat. The men floating in the icy water, often wounded or badly burned, knew this well. They expected no help except from the rescue ship, that hospital nurse of the seas, who like Kipling's water boy brought salvation to the survivors of shipwrecks. But where was the ship detailed for this purpose in the convoy? Perhaps she too had been sunk.*

Motionless, with ashen faces, the men stood there in silence, united as they had never been before. Doudet the merchant captain, Langlais the adventurer, O'Leary the doctor who had become a special agent, Archibald the ex-pilot, O'Neill, Fontenay, Rogers, Ferguson, Richardson . . . They stared into the distance at those black dots which they still seemed to see although they had disappeared from view. Abandoned shipmates.

They sailed towards the fine weather. The surviving ships had regrouped to sail in company to Gibraltar. Gliding through the ports, the morning sun brought to life the brass in the wardroom where O'Leary was breakfasting alone after his watch. Now the ship belonged to him. This knowledge had gradually dawned but for the past few days O'Leary had been certain. Something now bound him to the *Fidelity*. The Belgian now knew the ship's moods, caprices and weaknesses almost as well as Rogers. He heard her panting, smelled her odours and knew exactly how she settled down on the waves as though to sleep, or rode athwart the choppy swell until she was tired. But by a thousand details he also knew that the ship understood him. Day after day she had surrendered her secrets – the corner where the wind dropped miraculously and where one could stand upright while everything around was blown and tossed about. Protection from the waves, the refuge against the cold; the little hiding place away from inquisitive eyes or the importunate sympathy of comrades . . .

Despite this connivance O'Leary would never be a sailor. For him the *Fidelity* was only a means of transport, a way of going into battle. No more. Perhaps it was this mutual freedom

* Fourteen or fifteen units were sent to the bottom in this convoy, including the rescue ship.

between the man and the ship which had encouraged their mutual confidences.

O'Leary pushed back his plate and went into the galley.

'What about the skipper's breakfast?'

'I won't serve it to him.'

The night before a lively quarrel had broken out between Polo, the cook, and Lalande, the lieutenant with the birthmark on his face. The latter had reproached the cook for not keeping the coffee hot for the morning watch, Langlais had supported the young officer, and since then the cook had been livid.

'You mustn't be like that,' said the Belgian. 'Light your ovens and get the breakfast ready. You know that if the skipper doesn't get his in his cabin at half-past seven there'll be trouble.'

The cook shook his head.

'There may be trouble, but I won't serve him with his breakfast.'

Irritated, O'Leary went outside to smoke a cigarette. The air was cool and seemed to be gilded by the sun. The deck had never looked so peaceful or so tidy. He might have been on a cruise.

At ten minutes past seven he returned to the fray.

'Now what about that breakfast?'

'No.'

Anxious to avoid any trouble, O'Leary climbed the companionway leading to Langlais' quarters and knocked at the door.

'What's up?' asked the Corsican from his bunk.

'Your breakfast will be a little late, sir. We can't get the stove going.'

'Well, use the bellows and leave me in peace.'

O'Leary returned to the galley and walked over to Polo.

'I've told him breakfast will be late,' he said. 'You've still got time to get everything ready.'

'I've already told you I won't serve him his breakfast.'

Like all pusillanimous people who try to take a firm stand, the cook kept up his spirits by repeating his threats. At the end of the argument O'Leary shrugged his shoulders and left the wardroom. At a quarter to eight Langlais appeared on the companionway, in pants with a towel round his neck.

'Mortiss,' he roared. 'Where's Mortiss?'

At the bottom of the steps his eyes fell on Polo who had at last decided to do his duty and was lighting the stove.

'What the hell are you playing at?'

'I'm lighting the fire, sir,' said the man.

'At this time?'

'Yes, I told the second in command I didn't want to serve your breakfast.'

'What?'

Langlais could not believe his ears, but he did not ask the man to repeat his remark. With a bound he was in the galley.

'So you didn't want to serve my breakfast, eh?'

It was a mixture of amazement, incredulity and rage.

'Answer me.'

He seized the cook by the waist, hitched him on to the oven which was already warm and, despite the unfortunate man's screams, tried to sit him down on top of it. Hearing his cries, O'Leary appeared.

'Sir, sir! . . .'

Langlais was fuming with rage. His towel had slipped on to the stove and was scorching. Naked, suntanned, covered with scars, the skipper looked like a hairy gnome shaking a scarecrow.

'You'll see, Mortiss!' he roared. 'You'll see whether he smells like grilled pork or not!'

The cook yelled each time he came in contact with the burning metal. His trousers and apron were singed. In the distance it looked as though Langlais was raising the lid of a washing machine.

'Well, say it . . . Say it!' cried Langlas. 'I want to hear you say it . . . "I'm proud to take breakfast to the captain." '

'I am proud to take breakfast to the captain,' the unhappy man blurted out.

At last Langlais put him down on the ground.

The following day the *Fidelity* received her orders by radio. She did not reply for fear of divulging her position to the enemy. O'Leary learned at last that the fifteen Englishmen who had come on board at Greenock were secret agents. They had been chosen for their perfect knowledge of English and kept in the greatest secrecy. This explained their reserved attitude during the trip. The ship left the convoy and set course for Gibraltar. Where would these mysterious passengers go after that? To Africa, to Spain? The *Fidelity's* crew never knew.

Flying the White Ensign, the sailors lining the *Fidelity* proudly entered Gibraltar Harbour. Ten months before, she had slipped in like a foreigner and demanded protection. Today she had received her baptism of fire, and she was greeted as one of the few survivors of a sorely tried convoy. On the bridge, Doudet and Langlais stood side by side. Suspicious of each other or reconciled? Barclay, who had been almost invisible since they left, had joined them. A strange trio which seemed to have no really deep bonds. Were they even waging the same war? Doudet was in it more from loyalty to his ship than from personal conviction. Barclay followed Langlais. Thirst for vengeance, greed, passion? Perhaps a little of all three. And the skipper himself thought of nothing except serving his country.

The *Fidelity* was not to stay long in Gib. As soon as she had landed her guests, the skipper ordered water, coal and provisions to be taken on, then he reported to the Admiralty, accompanied by O'Leary. The barbed wire, the sentry on guard at the door, the clean ceiling and the corridor leading to Brown's office were unchanged. Leaving his second in command at the door, Langlais went in to see the British officer. He came out an hour later escorted by two strangers, each of them carrying a suitcase.

The three men made their way down the main street which, at this time of day, lay inert in the sun, without exchanging a word. They seemed to be hastening to some appointment.

CHAPTER NINE

SPECIAL MISSION

One of the passengers was a Maltese called Aromatic; the other was a Pole whose name no one ever discovered. They were installed in separate cabins and then, at about five o'clock, the captain gave orders to the engineer to light the boilers. They put to sea at night with all navigation lights extinguished. It was the 24th April, 1941.

This flight in the dark drew the attention of a port authority launch which set out in pursuit of the ship. Langlais ordered full steam ahead. The launch approached and with an Aldis lamp ordered the *Fidelity* to stop.

'The bloody fool,' roared Langlais. 'He'll get us spotted.'

He had to make up his mind to break radio silence and ask the port authorites to recall their vessel. The launch slowed down, put about and made for home. A few minutes later the Rock itself was engulfed by the night.

Langlais sent for O'Leary and the Belgian realized that the hour had come.

'Sit down,' said the skipper.

They could feel the Mediterranean lashing against the sides. The throb of the engines made the jug of water on the table rattle. The conversation lasted half an hour. When O'Leary left he sent for the 'hunchback.'

Apart from Doudet and Fontenay, he was the only real sailor aboard. A fair-haired Breton with a weather-beaten face and sleepy eyes, he was one of those men who always want to make sure that he understands before carrying out an order. He made the officer repeat his instructions three times although he had understood them from the start, then he saluted and said: 'Ay, ay, sir. I'll pipe Action Stations at 10.15 hours. Everything will be ready.'

He returned to his bunk.

The *Fidelity* continued to pant on her way in the darkness. O'Leary still had an hour's leisure in front of him and he spent it in his cabin. On board two hundred men were asleep. Only three privileged individuals knew that the signal would be given. It was given at 10.15. From the bridge O'Leary gave orders that the ship was to be entirely repainted. The hunchback had prepared pots of yellow paint, the rope ladders and cradles on which the sailors could slip down the sides of the ship. In a few hours the *Fidelity* was to be transformed into a Portuguese ship of 2,500 tons – the *Setubal* – which would be inconspicuous in these waters. In his cabin Langlais had a complete list of the silhouettes of neutral ships of a similar size and tonnage to the *Fidelity*. The camouflage had to be carried out at night with great care in order to avoid unpleasantness in case of a meeting with a prowling enemy U-boat. Certain lower structures which did not exist on the model had to be masked and others which the *Fidelity* did not possess to be improvised and, above all, she had to be painted from the waterline to the masthead.

On O'Leary's orders the sailors unscrewed the panels which had been installed in Barry, put hoods on the guns and erected false wooden installations. Others, sitting on wooden cradles half-way up the ship, painted with great strokes of the brush. Everyone was busy, from Barclay, who had come out of her cabin in a pair of jeans, to the ship's boy who fetched and carried.

Everyone scrubbed vigorously and the paint, which was purposely fluid, flowed down the flanks of the ship like trickles of sap.

'Don't go below the red line,' ordered Langlais, who was rushing to and fro, not afraid of getting his hands dirty.

Those who were painting the top of the hull formed a chain to supply their comrades below. The men outboard could feel the cold sea breeze on their legs. Painting large areas in the dark brings surprises. People painted several times over the same spot and left some of the panels completely bare. After five hours' work the ship looked like nothing in earth – neither the *Fidelity* nor the *Setubal*. She looked like a mildewed hulk just raised from the water.

Doudet stood powerless, watching the massacre of his ship.

'Complete lunacy,' he kept muttering between his teeth.

Archibald stared at him with curiosity. 'Strange man,' he said to himself, 'the air of the Mediterranean doesn't seem to agree with him.'

Perhaps the old sailor sensed the nearby French coast to the north and imagined that the *Le Rhône* was following her old route. But instead of sailing openly laden with vegetable oils, cocoa beans and coffee, she was now crawling along the Spanish coast under a mask like a thief.

Doudet had his own simple peasant morality which imposed certain obligations but no problems. A ship was a sacred pledge. The man who was in charge of her was answerable to his company. In case of ship wreck he was the last to leave the vessel. His duty was well defined but the regulations of the Merchant Navy had never foreseen the particular set of circumstances in which he now found himself. Sometimes he must have felt an urge to reassert himself, to go and threaten Langlais in his usurped cabin and insist upon the return of his ship to her home port. But was this the place to do it? Doudet would undoubtedly have been horrified at the idea of being a traitor. Besides, with his feverish patriotism, Langlais was capable of everything. Doudet had already seen him in action. In an outburst of rage he could have been quite capable of felling the ex-captain who had come to settle accounts. Doudet had no wish to die.

Dawn broke at about five o'clock. It heralded its appearance by a pale streak on the horizon, then by a faint orange lividness which spread suddenly over the sky. Balanced on trestles, Fontenay supervised the camouflage of the funnel. Lower down, balancing on the end of a rope, O'Leary guided Richardson who was painting the ship's name on the hull, *Setubal – Lisboa*. Archibald was tracing the nationality on the hatches. Spattered with yellow to the roots of her hair, Barclay seemed at the end of her tether. She had worked like a man all night. Now, sitting on a chest, she was taking a rest. She looked like a convalescent. O'Leary was struck by her gentle expression when he came up on deck. Without knowing the motive, he fetched a deck chair and set it up for her. Was she surprised or moved? Did she regret that she had shown signs of exhaustion? In any case, she did not thank him.

At six o'clock Langlais lowered a boat. The men rowed a few hundred yards away from the ship and made a tour round it so that the captain could gain some impression of the work as a whole. The night's work left much to be desired. In numerous places the paint had run and mingling with leakages of oil, had made dark trickles on the hull. The name did not stand out clearly. The funnel was not staggered at the same angle as that of the *Setubal*. The crew began to put the finishing touches and to get rid of all traces of their work.

'We're not finished yet,' said Langlais. 'The *Setubal* is a mixed cargo. I must have passengers, male and female.'

There was a burst of laughter from the men. The captain threw a key to the hunchback. 'Go down to cabin 10. You'll find a big wicker basket. Bring it up.'

O'Leary opened it. It was full of dresses, hats and men's suits. The men looked at each other open-mouthed. They were covered from head to foot with yellow paint and unshaved. It could be seen that they had not slept. The Barbary pirates who scoured the Mediterranean two hundred years before must have looked rather like them. They too must have stood open-mouthed, with legs apart to keep their feet in the rolling ship, as their prizes were opened.

'I want three men and two women,' said the captain.

The men nudged each other and laughed. There was a lot of obscenity. Barclay had returned to her cabin. O'Leary had to choose his actors at random. 'You and you – yes you, there – you're not bad looking.'

Eyes were turned on Marcelac, the frail young airman whom Langlais always teased and threatened to drown with his own hands. O'Leary pointed to him.

'Oh, no,' said Langlais. 'Not him – he'd enjoy it too much!'

The men donned their new garb.

At about 10 o'clock in the morning they went fishing with hand grenades. This was certainly an unusual occurrence in a mixed Portuguese cargo but, apart from that, the *Fidelity* was now camouflaged to perfection. Some Spanish fishing boats approached without noticing anything unusual. They continued to advance and the crew wondered what their goal was. The ship was under radio silence and Rogers confined himself to taking down shortwave messages which Langlais himself deciphered. The two genuine passengers did not appear.

Towards midday a Lufthansa seaplane – on the Paris–Madrid run via the Balearics – flew over the vessel. Did it find anything unusual which had not appeared when viewed from the sea? It circled the *Fidelity* before turning on a northerly course. This aroused questions on board. The bogus passengers began to get bored in their deck chairs and stood up to stretch their legs. Aware how ridiculous they looked, those in female garb hastily sat down again. If the German aircraft had noticed the characteristic shape of a gun battery despite the pains taken to hide it, a German fighter bomber would soon be paying them a visit. What would action be like in a ship covered with awnings, collapsible flats and bright-coloured deck chairs?

Rogers continued to receive messages and Langlais did not leave the wireless cabin. About six o'clock he sent for Aromatic and the Pole; and just before dinner announced to O'Leary: 'There will be a landing near Nice . . .'

He then retired to his cabin and Daladier served him with his dinner. That evening the actors, now useless, were allowed to change into their ordinary rig. Doudet had not uttered a word since morning. Exhausted by his supervision of the night work, he had taken an afternoon siesta. O'Leary took a delight in telling him that a raid was planned on the coast and to spice the story added: 'I think the captain intends to let us have a crack at a German cruiser.'

From that moment Doudet had lived in trepidation.

'Mortiss!'

Langlais' voice was serious. In the darkness his stocky frame was outlined against the greyish background of the passage. O'Leary followed him to the wardroom where Barclay was already seated.

'The show's for tonight,' said the captain. 'We're landing the two passengers near Perpignan and going a little further along the coast to take aboard fifteen specialist workers from the Skoda works.'

The Belgian's eyes lit up. 'Well, at last,' he said.

'The operation has to be rigorously timed,' went on Langlais. 'While I carry out the mission, you're in charge of the ship. If I don't return, you're to take the *Fidelity* back to Gib where you'll be given your orders.'

The second-in-command's face fell. 'Aren't I going with the landing?'

'No.'

'But captain,' protested O'Leary, 'you can't carry out this operation yourself. If it fails, the *Fidelity* would be lost. It only exists because you're on board, as you know only too well.'

'I'm not used to having my orders criticized,' replied

Langlais. 'This is our first mission and I want to carry it out myself.'

Normally, O'Leary bowed to his captain's decision but this time he was determined to oppose him.

'But you haven't the right to do it, sir. What would happen if, by some unlucky chance, you failed to return aboard? Doudet would take possession of the ship again.'

'Would you let him?'

'None of us are sailors and he knows that. You've only got to be away for a couple of days before he thinks he's the master again and takes on the airs of a swashbuckler. You're the only one who holds the threads of our fate in your hands. If you were to disappear everything would collapse.'

Barclay interrupted: 'You're right. If you leave the ship, Uncle's won the game.'

Langlais hesitated. They felt that he was jittering with excitement at the idea of the danger involved in landing on French soil, but the arguments of his two faithful supporters had thrown him off his balance. O'Leary fired a Parthian shot.

'If you leave us the *Fidelity* will become an ordinary cargo boat as she was before.'

'Don't talk bull, Mortiss,' the other burst out. 'If that old twat took over my boat I'd come back as a ghost and strangle him.' Then he shrugged his shoulders and said: 'Good. Well, you'll go.'

O'Leary chose his partners. Firstly Rogers, second-in-command of the commando team, and secondly Poëno, known as the 'Monster', an experienced fisherman and a competent mariner, invariably with a quid of tobacco in his mouth, who would bring the boat safely alongside, and finally Ford and Ferguson. He sent for the four men and told them to be ready at midnight. A few minutes later the *Fidelity* stopped about two miles from the shore.

Langlais left the radio post and rejoined his second-in-command at the rail. Now that the engines were silent the water could be heard lapping gently against the hull. Opposite they could see the intermittent flashes of a lighthouse. Fontenay, after consulting his charts, identified it as being Barcarès.

'You see that beam?' said Langlais. 'That's Barcarès, south of the Etang de Leucate. You'll land Aromatic and his mate there. Take two bicycles with you in the launch. It wasn't arranged but they might need them. From there, you'll turn south and sail along the coast. You have to be in Collioure before sunrise. A man will be waiting for you at the end of the breakwater. He'll be wearing a red scarf. You'll ask him "Which is the way to Montpellier?" and he will reply "I don't know. I'm a stranger in these parts." He will be the leader of the fifteen fellows we have to take on board. You'll embark them and set course for the open sea. The *Fidelity* will be waiting for you two and a half miles off shore.'

The launch was a heavy Breton ketch, an unusual sight in these waters, equipped with a 5 h.p. engine, a collapsible mast and lead weights as ballast. It had been tended very carefully during the journey, each part being verified regularly; the crew, surprised by this solicitude, had nicknamed it 'the sailors' cradle.' Two bicycles, a transmitting set, a few packages and a veritable arsenal were placed aboard. Langlais wanted his landing team to be in a position to defend itself in case of an unfortunate encounter.

He had armed it with two Lewis guns, four Thompson submachine-guns, seven 7·65 Colts, one per man, and fifty hand grenades. The boat was secured to the derrick. It was midnight. One after the other, Rogers, the 'Monster', Ferguson and Ford climbed into it. O'Leary followed, accompanied by Aromatic and the Pole. They looked like a boating party leaving. No one spoke except to give some necessary order. This departure was like an amputation. Suspended in their canoe, the men were now only attached to the *Fidelity* by ropes. It only remained to cut these.

A small group had collected around the boat – Langlais, Mamadou, Barclay, Archibald, O'Neill, Fontenay and the engineer.

'Barclay!' Langlais called out suddenly. 'Bring me your jewel case.'

It seemed an unusual request at such a moment, but the captain had procured cyanide pastilles in Liverpool and had entrusted them to Barclay; the girl had put them among her jewellery. Now he distributed them to the men taking part, giving them the poison like a communion wafer. The gesture was out of proportion to the danger run. The landing was to take place in the unoccupied zone far from direct contact with the enemy. But, on the one hand, Langlais did not know the conditions existing in Unoccupied France and, on the other, he always had a weakness for melodrama.

The boat touched the water. There was a lapping and the Monster switched on and pressed the starter. Once . . . twice . . . a dozen times. The engine coughed like a sick man and at each jerk the small boat banged against the side of the ship. Leaning over the rail, Langlais grew impatient.

'Well, can't you get it started?'

After a few more attempts the Breton announced: 'It's no good. I shall run the battery down.'

This delayed separation seemed onimous. Fate seemed to be telling them by a host of signs: 'Don't go.'

But Langlais did not see it in this light . . . 'Where's the engineer?' he roared. The man was standing behind him, trembling with fright. The captain jostled Mamadou out of the way and clutched the man responsible by the throat. 'So that's how you look after the launch, eh? I told you, you'll answer for it with your head.'

Losing control of himself, he banged the man's head against the side and tried to strangle him with his powerful hands.

'If the expedition fails,' he spluttered, 'I shall have you court-martialled.'

O'Leary had climbed up the rope ladder.

'Go and get the engine going,' he ordered the engineer.

His voice was firm. The fate of the mission was now in his hands and he knew that it was too late to dismiss the others.

The repair took an hour. At last the engineer climbed aboard and O'Leary went down the ladder. The ropes were cast loose and the seven men left. Rogers was at the tiller.

It was moonlight and the canoe leaped over the waves. Five hundred yards from the shore they switched off the engine. For a few seconds the 'sailors' cradle,' delivered to its own devices, rocked heavily until the Monster and Ferguson caught hold of the oars.

'It's going to be bloody tough work,' they swore as they bent to their task.

The handlebars of the bicycles gleamed. Ford covered them with the jackets which the rowers had discarded. The crossing seemed interminable. O'Leary, Rogers, Ford, Aromatic and the Pole listened for the least noise coming from the shore. When they were close in, the rowers shipped their oars and the tang of the sea rose in the boat.

'Come on,' said O'Leary.

He was the first to slip into the water. It was black and cold. He felt it enter his shoes, damp his trousers to his legs and cover his belly. He found a foothold on sand.

'Get up on my shoulders,' he ordered Aromatic.

The agents must not be allowed to get wet. At sunrise they had to mingle with the population and the stains of sea water would betray them. Imitating his superior, Rogers took charge of the Pole. The porters floundered. As soon as they were on dry land, their waterlogged shoes began to squelch. There was silence on the shore. Not a sound except the rustle of a few reeds in the wind. O'Leary and Rogers set out on a second trip. They carried the bicycles, radio and the bundles ashore. Now it was time to leave.

They shook hands and once more the Belgian and his companion entered the water. As the boat drew away, the silhouettes of the two agents were swallowed up in the darkness. Where were they going? What mysterious meetings had been planned for them? What perils would they face?

Suddenly they heard cries. The oars remained suspended in the air. Instinctively hands clutched weapons. It was nothing. It was simply that they had set their men down on one of these small tongues of land surrounded by water which are so common between Perpignan and Narbonnne. They were prisoners of the sea and the lake. In any other circumstance they would merely have had to wade through a few yards of low stagnant water on the top of which white solidified foam floated like flowers on the surface of fermented wine. They would then have found themselves on firm ground, stinking of the marsh and soaked to the calves. But their orders were clear. They had to reach the village without the slightest trace of their clandestine journey.

The canoe put about.

O'Leary and Rogers had to repeat, in the reverse direction, the two trips to re-embark the agents and their material. When they were safely aboard, they rowed off to find some more hospitable spot on the coast. This time, anxious to avoid a long trip for the porters, the Monster brought the boat close inshore. The manoeuvre was repeated. Soaked to the waist, the Belgian and his second-in-command shivered. When the last load had been deposited on the bank, they hurried back to the ship. Bicycles in hand, Aromatic and the Pole disappeared behind a bed of reeds.

'Make it snappy,' ordered O'Leary. 'Get the engine going.'

He would have to take a risk to make up the time lost. But the boat was stuck fast on the sandbank; the blocked screw refused to turn.

'Try again.'

Impossible.

The men began to grow nervous. Dawn would come up in an hour. The Belgian felt the cold and damp penetrate his belly.

'Come on, let's try once more.'

The preceding attempts had only made the screw bury itself more deeply in the mud. Getting purchase on the slippery ground, they tried to push the canoe off while the Breton functioned the engine. It was a waste of time. Then they plunged into the water up to their chests and tried to haul her off. Nothing doing. 'We must lighten her,' said Rogers.

The men worked feverishly. The useless thwarts were jettisoned, followed by the gratings and the oars. Finally, the mast went overboard.

'It's not enough,' said the Monster, after another attempt with the self-starter. 'Take out a couple of the lead weights.'

There were six in all and they were heavy. It took several attempts before the first two could be jettisoned. Even then the screw would not turn. Ferguson tried to hollow out the mud round it with the end of his oar.

'We've been here three-quarters of an hour,' said O'Leary.

One after the other, the four bars of lead were sacrificed.

'If we ever manage to leave we're going to be tossed about like a cork,' said Rogers. Finally, pushed, dragged and shaken, the canoe was freed from its muddy prison. At full speed it set out for Collioure, throwing up a wake of spray.

CHAPTER TEN

PAT O'LEARY

'We shall be at least two hours late.'

His face bathed in sweat, O'Leary cursed the bad luck which now forced the little team to carry out its mission in broad daylight. He was worried about the men who were waiting for them.

'Perhaps they've gone.'

With the sunrise, the north wind began to blow; the unballasted boat bobbed on the waves and shipped a great deal of water.

'Shall I hug the coast, sir?' asked the Monster.

The Belgian agreed and they continued on their course 25 yards from the shore. After leaving Argelès, the coast changed. The long, flat expanses gave place to rocky escarpments beneath which the canoe found comparative calm. It was five o'clock in the morning. While out to sea, the Mediterranean sparkled, in the creeks which the sun had not yet penetrated it seemed flat.

'Collioure,' Ford announced curtly.

O'Leary had expected a blaze of colours. At first he could see nothing but a yellowish dyke jutting out into the sea, but as they drew closer the round tower on the mole appeared, a little inland. The shore masked the village itself. O'Leary was looking for the figure of a man standing on the end of the breakwater, a man wearing a red scarf. He was there. The passengers must have waited. A few turns of the screw and the canoe was within hailing distance.

'The route for Montpellier,' roared O'Leary, between two rockings.

'I don't know, I'm a stranger to these parts,' replied the man.

The words were uttered in a sing-song southern voice without a trace of impatience. 'We thought you weren't coming,' he said. 'What happened to you?'

'Where are the others?' asked the Belgian anxiously. He had to hold on to the wales in order not to fall. The wind carried his remark away.

'The what?'

'The others.'

'Oh, the others. They've gone back to bed. I'll go and fetch them.'

The men in the canoe could not believe their ears. Armed to the teeth, nerves on edge, they had been prepared for a raid and had found at the meeting-place disappointed tourists who, when they did not arrive, had calmly gone back to bed. O'Leary was furious.

'I give you five minutes,' he roared, 'If you're not back in five minutes we shall leave without you.'

It was now broad daylight. The tower of the mole stood out against the pale sky. They could distinguish the ochre patina of its crown of russet tiles. One after the other the stones of the dyke lit up. They circled a few cable lengths off shore for nearly twenty minutes. At last the messenger returned. This time he was out of breath.

'They're coming,' he declared. 'Wait another quarter of an hour.'

'Impossible,' cried Roger, 'the boat's rocking too much.'

'Enter the harbour. You've nothing to fear.'

The five men exchanged glances.

'Don't do it,' advised Polëno. 'It smells fishy to me.'

'Go in,' ordered O'Leary.

Fishermen were lined up on the inner wall of the jetty, their legs dangling and their lines in the sea. They looked apathetically at the boat which, after rounding the pebbles, entered the old port. In the distance were the pastel-coloured houses just as O'Leary had imagined; he could read the inscriptions on their façades. Epicerie, Bar Tabac, Souvenirs, and the names of the fishing boats which rubbed their hulls against each other from the wake of the canoe. Brown fishing nets were drying against the walls like gigantic spiders' webs. On the quay were a few early morning strollers in rope-soled shoes. Some of them stopped to shake hands with the others. No one appeared to have the slightest interest in the canoe, which, with its throttled engine, was circling in the middle of the roadstead.

'If it goes on like this, I'm going ashore to get a packet of Gauloises,' said Ford.

'You're mad – they're rationed,' replied Ferguson.

O'Leary was growing impatient.

'What the hell are they up to? If they don't turn up soon we shall have to leave.'

'Yes, let's take a powder,' said Rogers.

The Monster began to accelerate the motor when a voice cried out: 'What are you up to there?'

It was a Customs official who had come out of the Bar Tabac.

'We're fishing,' cried O'Leary. Then, turning to the man at the helm, ordered: 'Full speed ahead.'

At that moment the man with the red scarf appeared on the breakwater with a dozen travellers carrying bundles. The Customs officer signalled the canoe to come alongside.

'I want to see your papers.'

'Have we got time to take these lascars aboard?' O'Leary asked Rogers.

'No. Besides – look! They're leaving again. We've flunked it.'

'Are you taking the mickey out of me?' shouted the irate Customs official. 'Bring me your papers at once or I'll telephone the police.'

'All right, all right. We're coming,' said the Belgian, and then to his crew: 'Let's get out of here.'

The boat leapt towards the open sea. The fishermen on the jetty saw it pass below in a jet of spray. Furious, the mystified Customs official had run into the café to telephone. The man in the red scarf and his companions had disappeared from the breakwater. A swell was now running. Lightened beyond the limits of prudence, the canoe took the waves athwart and fell off balance into the trough. Clutching on to the stern, O'Leary watched the hill, the castle on the rock, the Miradoux fort and the operetta setting of the port disappear . . .

They were a mile off shore when the motor stopped. There was a strong smell of petrol.

'What's wrong?' growled Ferguson.

The tank was in the bows; a copper pipe joined it to the motor. With the jolting it had become unsoldered and the spirit had leaked into the bottom of the boat. They were floundering in a mixture of salt water and petrol.

'It's had it,' said the Monster.

O'Leary knelt in the liquid and with icy hands tried to arrest the flow with his handkerchief. At each jolt his numbed fingers were torn on the metal. Without motive power, the canoe received resounding slaps from the waves.

'It's holding,' said the Belgian, standing up. 'Get out the cans.'

To put in petrol with a north wind blowing and you are unsteady on your legs seems an impossibility. Supporting each other, Rogers and the Monster tried to direct the capricious jet towards the mouth of the tank. At the least gust of wind, the least wave, they lost control of the can and sprayed the backs of their mates. Moreover, in contact with the air the petrol evaporated. It got into their eyes and throats. They could not see and they kept on spitting petrol-tasting saliva. Three cans were used. Some of the petrol went into the tank but most of it was lost in the sea.

'Contact!' ordered O'Leary.

Lying on his belly in the slime, Ford held the binding on with his hand, to prevent the ship's lifeblood from flowing. The Monster started the engine and Rogers took the tiller. They set out again. Five hundred yards later a wave more violent than the rest flung Ford into the bottom of the boat. The petrol spurted from the damaged pipe and the engine stopped.

O'Leary seized the torn handkerchief and retied the knots. The petrol flowed on to the scratches on his palms and made his mouth feel sticky. He felt like vomiting.

'Come on,' he cried.

The engine started again. At that moment Ferguson roared: 'A launch . . .' Growing larger at every second it was bearing down on them.

'Faster – they're catching us!'

O'Leary's hands were numb. He did not even turn round to see if his pursuers were gaining ground. He was merely a piece of soldering on a pipe. In that resided their last chance of safety. At a particularly brutal jolt the repairs broke once more and the last of the petrol flowed into the canoe

'I told you – we've had it,' said the Monster.

The enemy was upon them. In the bows of the launch they could see a man in blue uniform with a rifle in his hand.

'Where are you making for?'

O'Leary heard the question above the din of the waves.

'We've broken down,' he explained, pointing to the two ends of the broken pipe.

The coastguard still had his rifle trained on the occupants of the boat. His mate uncoiled a rope to cast to them.

'That's it – we've had it,' said Rogers. 'They're going to tow us into port.'

On the first occasion, the Belgian pretended to miss the proffered rope. He was gaining time and thinking hard.

No petrol, no mast. It was therefore quite impossible to rejoin the *Fidelity*. To fight – what was the point? The

weapons were soaked and the canoe could not manoeuvre. No –
they were caught. No – the important thing was to hide the
presence of the camouflaged ship in these waters.

O'Leary caught the rope.

'Take us back to the shore,' he said.

In the boat, consternation reigned.

'They'll fling us in jail.'

'Worse than that – they'll hand us over to the Boches.'

O'Leary told them his plan.

'In no circumstance must we admit that we belong to an
English boat. Not a word about the *Fidelity*. We're civilians . . .
French prisoners of war who have escaped from Germany and
were trying to join de Gaulle. We stole this canoe to try and
reach Spain.'

'Where did we steal it?'

'We must refuse to say.'

Ploëno shook his head. 'What about the weapons?'

'We must throw them overboard.'

Towed by the launch, they sped over the water. Ferguson
and the Monster took up their position well in view in the bows.
They stood up despite the violence of the wind. Under cover of
their bodies, the three others began to get rid of the weapons.
Laboriously they hitched the heavy weapons on to the wale and
dropped them over the side. In the case of the Colts, it was
more simple. They flung them into the waves like pebbles.

The two boats were in sight of the shore when the rope
broke. Several attempts were necessary before they were in
harness again. They left at last and a little later Ford identified
the houses of Port-Vendres. The five seamen were naked and
defenceless. In a few minutes they would know what awaited
them.

A crowd had gathered round the sheds in the harbour. A Port-
Vendres-Algiers boat was tied up at the quayside. Bundles of
vegetables in wide-meshed nets were being unloaded by

derrick. There was a smell of oil and garlic. The soaking wet, grease-stained fugitives were surrounded by naval police as soon as they set foot ashore. There was no hostility; some of the bystanders started to jest.

'They've been picked up.'

'They must have been in a bloody hurry . . .'

The crowd is always cowardly. It never likes authority to be flouted. They jested among themselves in Catalan.

'They're taking the mickey out of us,' said Rogers angrily.

The gendarmes cleared a passage for them. O'Leary noticed an Italian officer among the civilians. One side of the harbour was occupied entirely by the Hôtel de la Compagnie du Midi. Two cars were waiting in the shade in front of the entrance. Both of them bore the notice: 'SP' on the windscreen. The captives seemed to be exploring a new world. On one of the façades they read an inscription in red, white and blue: 'A single leader – Pétain; a single method – the Legion; a single goal – France.' The importers discussed the price of the unloaded vegetables outside the cafés.

'I can't do anything about it, *mon vieux* – it's the taxes.'

Through the open windows came a smell of cooking. O'Leary realized that he was hungry.

The prisoners were taken to Naval Headquarters and shown into a captain's office. It was a damp, cold room covered with Vichy Government propaganda posters. Dripping with water like five clouts taken out of a wash basin, the sailors sat down in front of the officer.

'Well, gentlemen,' he asked, 'why did you not reply when the Customs Officer hailed you?'

'We were trying to escape,' O'Leary said firmly.

'Where were you going to?'

'To Spain and from there to England.'

The Belgian had decided to be violent. This alone would distract attention from the *Fidelity*. In his heart he hoped that by styling himself a de Gaullist he would be understood and perhaps even be given a little latitude. He described himself as the head of a small group of escaped prisoners of war who were trying to put themselves once and for all out of reach of the Germans. The captain listened to him without interruption. He even brought out a packet of cigarettes and handed them round to his visitors.

'You run no risk here,' he said. 'We're in the unoccupied zone. The occupation authorities have no say here.'

'I know,' replied O'Leary, 'but we preferred to go a bit further afield.'

The captain shrugged his shoulders.

'Gentlemen,' he said, 'I think that's cleared up everything. I can't do anything for you. I myself am a Lorrainer and I understand your feelings. But we have signed an armistice and it is my duty as an officer to respect the terms of it. Much to my regret, I shall have to arrest you.'

The Belgian had been expecting this for some moments. He felt almost relieved. It allowed him freedom of action again. From now on he would only think of how he could escape. The five men went into the neighbouring room where a big fire was burning. They were given hot coffee. Feeling slightly better, O'Leary was aware of his various aches and pains. His hands had been bruised from banging against the side of the canoe and the blisters had burst on his palms from rubbing against the pipe. And yet his right thigh hurt more than anything. He did not remember having injured it. Suddenly he realized – the burning sensation was due to the cyanide pastille in the pocket of his trousers. He took advantage of a change of clothes – a sailor had brought them in new garments – to remove all traces of the poison from the painful spot.

'Gentlemen,' said the sailor who had distributed the coffee, 'be good enough to follow me to the prison.'

Before leaving, he handed a military blanket to each of the men.

O'Leary went over to Rogers. 'Now it's every man for

himself and God for us all,' he whispered. 'Main objective to join the *Fidelity* at Gibraltar. Tell the others. I myself am going to have a shot.'

As a precaution, the sailor took only Ford and O'Leary with him and left the three others for a second trip. Outside the sun was shining. It was very hot and the road led to the village much higher up with its station directly overlooking the port. O'Leary carried his blanket over his right arm; skilfully thrown it would trip up the guard. Then he would only have to run fast . . .

Ford appeared to be interested in the view, and yet taking advantage of a moment's inattention on the part of the sailor, he exchanged glances with his chief.

We must wait till we get to the top of the hill and past the last houses, thought O'Leary.

In order to impart his plan, he moved over to the left. Port-Vendres was now well below them. They could still see the roofs of the sheds, the sign of the Hôtel de la Compagnie du Midi and the masts of the steamer, but the houses on the quayside had disappeared. O'Leary looked out to sea. Under the effect of the heat the horizon bathed in a silvery mist seemed to quiver. And suddenly the prisoner saw her . . .

At first he thought it was a mirage. Then he felt a cold shiver run down his spine. That curious lower structure, that yellow funnel, yes, it was the *Fidelity*.

'They're mad,' muttered O'Leary, his heart filled with gratitude.

Checking the blanket in the hollow of his elbow, he waited for the top of the hill . . .

On the bridge of the *Fidelity*, Langlais was roaring like a captive beast. 'They've murdered them or else they would be here.'

Towards midday it was obvious that the expedition had been a failure and the skipper reluctantly gave orders to sail for

Gibraltar. Everyone was silent on board. It was a gloomy meal; there were too many empty seats. Pushing back his plate, Langlais retired to the wireless cabin where Rogers was no longer there to receive messages. An hour later he came out with a frown on his face: 'Archie,' he called.

Each gesture stressed some absence and created a new hierarchy.

'At eight o'clock you'll assemble the crew. We've got to repaint the ship. If Mortiss and his men have been captured there's every chance that we've been spotted. We must change our identity.'

This time the *Fidelity* was transformed into a Spanish ship belonging to a Barcelona-Palma company. The work was done listlessly by night. Not having slept for two days, most of the sailors were dropping with fatigue. The morale was low in the ship. The rumour ran round that she was being chased by an Italian patrol boat. Without the fact having been mentioned they were painting the *Fidelity* for battle.

At dawn Langlais repeated his inspection of the previous night. Painted in bright colours, the ship looked magnificent.

'You're getting your hand in, painters,' he cried, but the jest fell flat.

Insensitive to the excitement outside, Barclay had taken possession of the belongings of O'Leary, Rogers, Ferguson, Ford and Ploëno. She had spread them out brazenly on the wardroom table. The hunchback who had brought them in left the room in dusgust; when he arrived on deck he spat with contempt. Everything was going badly. After his rocket from Langlais, Mamadou wandered round the passages like a lost soul.

Langlais was coming down from his quarters when, from the top of the waxed stairs, he saw Barclay sorting the belongings of his commando team.

'What the hell are you doing with that?' There was a snarl in his voice and his hand was raised ready to strike.

She turned her tigress' eyes on him.

'We agreed that our belongings should be shared out twelve hours after our disappearance. I'm keeping my word.'

'But they don't belong to you.'

Barclay shrugged her shoulders. 'Don't you understand that if you don't replace them . . . in their cabins, in their jobs . . . in everything, you'll reduce the morale of the crew to zero. It's not pilfering, it's hygiene, that's all. When the others see that they've been forgotten, they'll shut their traps.'

This cold lucidity stupefied Langlais. He could only stutter ; . . 'But they made a will . . .'

'Well, what of it? How do you know they're dead?'

She was almost beautiful with the sun turning her hair to flame. Langlais had not the heart to smash his fist into her face.

'Bitch!' he shouted. He rushed out of the wardroom, slamming the door behind him.

At about two o'clock Fontenay, who was on watch, reported to the captain: 'Ship on the port bow.'

The vessel spotted was sailing a westerly course and its route would bring it across the *Fidelity*'s bows. Langlais took up his glasses. At his side Doudet scrutinized the intruder through a pair of old naval binoculars.

'If I'm not mistaken,' he said, 'we've just met ourselves.'

'What do you mean?' asked Langlais.

The merchant captain wiped his eyes and looked again.

'Yes – the ship we're supposed to be is sailing towards us,' he said.

In spite of his irritation Langlais could not help laughing. He changed course but it was too late to avoid recognition. The two ships passed within hailing distance of each other and the *Fidelity* hurriedly changed course.

'Their timetable must have been changed,' said Langlais. 'Normally she puts to sea twice a week.'

That evening they entered the Straits. The captain stopped

the engines and a third painting fatigue was ordered to return the ship to her original aspect. Almost dropping with fatigue, the hunchback protested: 'For Christ's sake, why don't they make up their minds ... Yellow, green, grey – they're taking the mickey out of us.'

Langlais had heard him. When the sailor appeared in the passage, carrying a bucket in each hand, he found the captain barring his way.

'Put those down,' ordered the captain.

The man obeyed.

'And take that on your snout to teach you not to criticize my orders,' he said, hitting him hard in the face.

The following day the *Fidelity* entered the harbour. She was as grey as on the day she had sailed. Her sailors lined the decks and the White Ensign was flying on the poop. She was lacking only a canoe and five men.

CHAPTER ELEVEN

BLOODY ENCOUNTER

'She bored me. She never stopped asking me questions.

' "Do you like anchovy toast, commander? Or do you prefer it with Chester?" Finally I couldn't stick it any longer. I stuffed my hand in her goldfish bowl, picked out her prize Japanese specimen, stuffed it between two slices of bread and ate it while it was still quivering. After that she left me in peace.'

Langlais was doubled up with laughter. This Gaullist sloop commander was a man after his own heart. He thought about nothing but boardings, the women he had laid and brawls. In actual fact, he was a borderline case and a few months later had to be sent to hospital. In the meantime he was a fine companion. His unit was tied up alongside the *Fidelity* in Liverpool Harbour and the two skippers were constantly inviting each other aboard. One evening, to show the discipline that reigned in his ship, Langlais posted armed sentries at each end of the passages. He pushed the joke so far as to post a steel-helmeted rating with a tommy-gun in the heads.

The *Fidelity*'s return to England had been marked by a number of pranks in very questionable taste. Renewed pilfering, fights provoked with Gaullist officers, revolver shots on the quayside, spectacular demonstrations and petty bravado. As soon as they berthed, Archibald had to hand over the explosives on board to the port authorities. Obeying the captain's orders, he had only delivered up a few depth charges and a dozen detonators carefully wrapped up in waterproof cotton wool. But in the drawer where he kept his shirts he still had about two thousand. Langlais and his pilot liked to feel that they possessed weapons which were not recorded on the Admiralty lists.

At Liverpool Doudet had resumed the lazy rhythm of his pre-war life. His trousers slack at the waist and a pipe in his mouth, he wandered about in his ragged vest looking for a shady corner or shut himself up in his cabin. He only appeared at meal times.

'Here's the old man with his mosquito net,' said Barclay. 'He must have smelt the grub.'

The 'old man' did not reply. Langlais' affairs did not seem to be going very well and Doudet was probably quite pleased. Like the others, he had succumbed to the Corsican's charm and submitted to his stern authority, but this submission did not prevent him from using his reason.

The mission on the French coast had resulted in a partial setback. They had landed two agents who, according to Langlais, had later established contact with the intelligence service and were doing good work in France. But the Collioure affair had stressed the hazardous character of similar operations. Moreover, they did not seem justified when one compared the results obtained with the means engaged; in order to land a dozen men it was pointless to use a ship like *HMS Fidelity*.

This obvious lack of proportion, which Langlais did not seek to justify, made things look bleak for the future. Mystery, which had once been Langlais' trump card, had now rebounded on himself.

'If he has any confidence in us, he ought to keep us informed as to what he's cooking,' Marcelac maintained in his high-pitched voice.

'If he really is preparing something,' replied Doudet, puffing at his pipe.

Archie listened to these recriminations in silence. Life appeared good to him as it was. His education had not provided for his living the life of a pirate among pots of paint and detonators, but although his presence on board was unusual, he was perfectly ready for any postponements. He rather enjoyed the idea, he said, with a wink, that things might turn out badly.

The tragedy began with a murky story of poisoned tinned foods destined for the enemy. Once more Langlais had refused to give any details of this diabolical plan.

'Store them away from the other provisions and let no one touch them.'

A few days later young Harrow fell seriously ill and had to be taken as an urgency case to hospital. It was whispered that the Corsican had wanted to get rid of an embarrassing witness. For several weeks Harrow had not hidden his views about what was going on on board the *Fidelity*. Some echo of his indignation might have reached Langlais' ears. In actual fact the boy was laid low by an acute appendix, which had nothing to do with either the captain or the tinned goods. In any case, the latter were never used.

The proportions this incident assumed showed the endemic unrest of the crew. Langlais pretended to ignore it. He realized how much he missed O'Leary. With the skill of a doctor, the Belgian had known how to diagnose the rise in temperature in the ship before it became dangerous, and as soon as he had made his diagnosis, he ordered the remedies without consulting the skipper.

Now that the quack was no longer there, Langlais had to look for other support. At first he apparently thought of Doudet. On the pretext of duty he often sent him to London. A room was reserved for him at the Mayfair and on his arrival Uncle found girls of easy morals ready to look after him. Fearing that the old salt would be indiscreet, Langlais had called upon women in the Secret Service to avoid this. Doudet did not seem to realize the organized nature of his good fortune and returned from London with a store of stories in which he always played the leading role.

'You're lucky to have found any English girls with a bit of temperament,' joked Langlais.

There was too great a gulf between them. The Corsican had usurped his command and his behaviour had been scandalous. Possibly Doudet had made up his mind to turn a blind eye, since there was nothing else he could do. Having little respect for this usurper, he at least accepted the material rewards which his painful situation obtained for him.

Barclay's thoughts seemed to run on the same lines. Intelligent and avaricious, she was bound to have seen through Langlais' game. Since the captain of the *Fidelity* was handling Doudet with kid gloves it meant that he needed him; moreover, in all probability he also needed her. From there to conclude that she could obtain her share was an easy step to cross for a clear-thinking feminine brain. She crossed it.

On the least occasion she demanded presents. Nothing was too good for her. She also knew how to make Langlais pay for the services she rendered him by keeping an eye open on everything on board. She was not in the least embarrassed by this rather degrading role of paid stool-pigeon. Anyhow, she never evinced any shame, and her love for Langlais must have justified herself in her own eyes.

The Corsican still treated her with possessive passion. One morning a British sailor forgot to salute the girl as she crossed the quay on her way to the ship. Langlais was on deck. He leapt ashore, flung himself on the sailor and struck him violently. Once more the 'little fellow' had to intervene to get the matter hushed up.

Although assured of Doudet and Barclay, Langlais had not yet replaced O'Leary. He must have hesitated a long time before choosing Fontenay. A different approach was necessary in his case. A very courageous regular officer, better educated than most of his shipmates, Fontenay admired his captain's patriotism but did not appreciate his behaviour. Certain of Langlais' eccentricities – the reestablishment of summary justice, the introduction of a bodyguard consisting of Daladier and Mamadou, the unorthodox presence of Barclay shocked him as a professional sailor and as a man of honour.

He had thought of leaving the ship and had confessed as much to Archibald, but the old cargo vessel with its tired engines and its overpainted hull had become too much part and parcel of his life; she had got under his skin. Like all the others, Fontenay felt at once with these worn-out decks, the hooded guns, the icy passages down which the wind whistled. As time went by, the *Fidelity* was Langlais' best trump. The crew were above all faithful to her.

Langlais put out some feelers. He told Fontenay that he had failed to pass his Naval examinations. Was it true? It is of little importance. Fontenay had sat for them. Thus a first bond was forged between the two men. Then Langlais admitted the existence of his Indo-Chinese son. Fontenay confessed that before he left Paris he had given his mistress a child. They exchanged photographs of their sons. Langlais had won the game.

Having made sure of his 'two sailors', Langlais flattered the crew by a series of spectacular gestures. Luck was on his side. Archie's servant, an ex-professional boxer, had beaten up a couple of British policemen in a brawl. He was arrested and sentenced to pay a fine of £4. Langlais exploited the incident to show that he stuck to his sailors. He climbed on to the bridge and before the assembled crew handed £20 to the hunchback to pay the man's fine and to reward a shipmate who had defended the honour of his ship so well.

But Langlais surpassed himself in the case of 'Piti Lapin.' The affair dated back to O'Leary's period. On one of his frequent outings in London with the Belgian, the captain had met a young protitute called 'Piti Lapin.' The evening had begun Chez Prunier. Langlais had shown that he was a gourmet and was as roysterous as usual. After a dispute about the bill he left in high spirits. From there the two men went to the Crocodile to drink a bottle of champagne. There Langlais noticed 'Piti Lapin.'

'Let's take her to Johnson's place,' he suggested to O'Leary.

Anxious to avoid any scandal in the hotels, Johns had fixed up the captain of the *Fidelity* and his companion in a boarding house directly controlled by his service at 92 Ebury Street. This extremely discreet and respectable house was run by a certain Mr. Johnson. The idea of bringing a woman into this haven of morality delighted O'Leary. An hour later three shadows tiptoed into Mr. Johnson's house.

Langlais was up the following morning at seven o'clock; he was shaving naked in front of the mirror.

'I'll see you at midday at the Regent Palace,' he said to his second in command, as soon as he was ready to leave.

Left alone, Mortiss sighed. He wondered how he was going to get 'Piti Lapin' out without arousing the attention of Mr. Johnson.

The girl in the other bed was beginning to wake up. She opened an eye, recognized the room and threw back the blankets.

'Listen,' said O'Leary, 'I'm going to ring for breakfast. Hide in the cupboard.'

The girl did as she was told. A few seconds later the valet brought in the tray. O'Leary gave him a friendly smile and accompanied him to the door. Everything was going all right until as he left the man trod on something. He bent down to pick up the object and with an air of disgust handed O'Leary a pink brassière.

'We've been spotted,' said the Belgian, unlocking the cupboard. 'Get dressed quickly.'

'Piti Lapin' slipped out through the window.

When the officers returned to Ebury Street at three o'clock in the afternoon their luggage was waiting in the hall. 'You asked for your bill, gentlemen. Here it is,' said Mr. Johnson. A bewhiskered valet hailed a taxi. The two undesirable guests were shown into it without a word of reproach.

'Piti Lapin' was a faithful type. Langlais was delighted to meet her again on his return from the mission. How did the idea enter his head to buy her services for the gratification of his crew? In any case, he proposed it to her without the least trace of shame.

'To a certain extent you'll be the godmother of the whole ship.'

Forgetting that the Marquise de C. had already given the *Fidelity* a more respectable godmother, Langlais assembled his men.

'Men,' he said, 'in future when you go to London, there'll be someone waiting for you. I've laid on a whore for you. Try and do honour to your ship.'

The crew had expected something else. Langlais had promised them action and they had been languishing in harbour for weeks. On the Continent the armies of the Reich were advancing across the Russian plains. In Africa Rommel was harassing the Eighth Army. News was rare from France – a few official messages forwarded by the Red Cross and from time to time a letter which arrived mysteriously via Spain or Switzerland. The raids on England continued. The morale of the *Fidelity* sank day by day.

Liverpool did not offer the same distractions as Barry; it was too big and they felt lost.

'Oh, for that little Cardiff train!' sighed O'Neill.

They used to take it during the week. It was winter, and since it did not stop between Barry and Cardiff the doors were locked when it left. This avoided a double ticket control and allowed them to transform each heated compartment into a bedroom on wheels.

Finally, at the beginning of July, Langlais returned from London wreathed in smiles.

'Gentlemen,' he said to the officers, 'we shall be leaving soon. This time it will be on a big mission with commandos, heavy weapons and air support.'

The captain's words were soon supported by facts. Once more the *Fidelity* underwent transformations. She was even given the *Surcouf*'s seaplane which Langlais entrusted to Marcelac. A mechanic was attached to him to service it. To replace 'the sailor's cradle' which had been lost off Collioure, a fast launch was hoisted aboard. Finally provisions, cigarettes, ammunition and spirits were lowered into the holds.

Langlais was jubilant.

A special ship, a special mission and special rations . . .

He sent Archibald to London with confidential documents for Smith.

'You're to show him these but you're to bring them back here.'

This was the first time the lieutenant had seen the 'little fellow'. Smith offered him a chair and a cigarette and then unsealed the envelope. Archie looked at the portrait of an RAF airman on the desk. Smith's son had been brought down by his own flak on his return from a mission.

'It's the war,' the 'little fellow' said simply.

When he had finished reading, he turned to the Frenchman. 'This is very interesting, I should like to keep these documents.'

'The captain told me to bring them back with me.'

'Oh, well, that's different. Come and have a cup of tea.'

Smith took his visitor into the next door room. Ten minutes later they returned to his office and Archie was given back his envelope, carefully sealed.

'Thank you, lieutenant, these documents have now been photographed.'

The *Fidelity* left Liverpool on the 30th August, 1941. With three agents from the Free French Forces on board, their desti-

147

nation was once more Gibraltar. They sailed in convoy. The monotonous watches began again, with WT signals between the boats reproaching them for stringing out. Long, uneventful nights . . . From time to time the duty watch brought them a sandwich and a cup of coffee. Although it was summer the nights were cold. The awnings had been erected and the officers brushed up their astronomy. All the officers had decided to let their beards grow and one bearded man after another climbed up to the bridge. When the time hung too heavy it was the tradition to twit the men in the engine room. They blew down the speaking tube and said: 'You're smoking down there.'

'Me?' came an indignant voice from the depths.

'Yes, you, I can see you.'

Then the relief watch arrived. He usually turned up five minutes before time, and one usually stayed on a little with him. And the monotonous life continued . . .

On the 1st September there was a submarine alert.

Langlais screamed his orders into the 'voice pipe' on the bridge. The men rushed to their action stations, lowered the mobile panels from the rail and loaded their guns.

'Those bloody guns,' swore Archibald. 'You can grease them every day, but one wave and the barrels are rusty.'

False alarm! Langlais tried to inform his lieutenant but the latter did not hear. Seizing the rifle which was within reach of his head, the captain aimed carefully at his steel helmet. The bullet richochetted off the metal with a whine. The officer gave a start under the shock and turned round.

'Well, can't you answer when I call you?' asked Langlais.

On another occasion he had fired at the crow's nest where the look-out man had fallen asleep. 'That'll bring him down,' he said. These brutalities were part of the aura he had built up around himself and which was supposed to be rumbustious. They did not please everyone. Commander V . . . despatched by the London Committee on a mission to Occupied France, a mess mate in the wardroom since they left, did not disguise how

much they irritated him. At table the incidents grew more frequent. Langlais was not the type of man to put up with oppo-
sition for long. One evening he brought the conversation round
to war and politics. He was didactic and passionate, a typical
dissenter. At first the passenger tried to avoid an argument, but
Langlais managed to get him on the raw.

'God said, "I loathe the Laodiceans".'

Irritated, the other replied aggressively. Langlais treated
him as a Pétain supporter and then embarked upon a pro-
British tirade. The Gaullist agent swallowed the bait. Langlais
struck.

'Leave the wardroom, sir, I will not allow any anti-British
propaganda in my ship.'

Commander V ... was placed under close arrest in his
cabin. A tragedy was brewing. It burst the following morning.
Archibald was on watch at eleven o'clock when the chief engineer passed, freshly shaved.

'Hallo, chum,' said Archie, 'have you at last found out where
your engines are?'

This was a standing joke. People on board maintained that
the chief engineer had never been down into the engine room
and that he did not even know its whereabouts.

'Not yet,' he retorted, 'you see, lieutenant, I'm looking
for ...'

'That was a shot.'

The noise came from a cabin not far from the wireless cabin.
Archibald remembered that Commander V ... was there
under arrest. Rushing down from the bridge, he hurried along
the passage. Other members of the crew were already there –
O'Neill, Fontenay, Harrow and Marcelac. They tried the door
but it was locked from inside. They called out but there was no
reply. Then they broke down the panel. The officer was lying in
his bunk, dead.

'He's killed himself,' said Fontenay, in a toneless voice.

The revolver had fallen to the ground.

This was the first death in the *Fidelity*.

No enemy bullet had struck him; it seemed that he had died for nothing. A moment later Archibald said to himself: 'Langlais has killed him.' In his intransigence, the captain would have been quite capable of this, but it was obviously a case of suicide. Everything confirmed this – the locked door, the position of the body and the character of the wound. Besides, if the skipper of the *Fidelity* had wanted to get rid of someone, he would have strangled him with his own hands and in broad daylight.

Nevertheless, the lieutenant could not help thinking that Langlais had liquidated the old soldier with a more murderous weapon than gunpowder. He had aroused doubts in his mind and had made him fear that he was a traitor. Neither the captain nor the agent were responsible for this tragedy; the officer was a casualty of the war, as he might have been of cancer, without outside interference.

Langlais ordered an inquest. Then he sent for Barclay.

'Arrange the ceremony, ma'am.'

Without more ado the body was confined to the depths.

Stained with blood, the voyage continued in the sunshine. In the wardroom the men tried to banish the boredom of hours at sea with lengthy games of cards. Langlais cheated, as usual. If he lost, he got up, pushed back the table and went down to his cabin. One day he tore up a pack of cards. Barclay played to please him, but at the least mistake she was sworn at. At meals, corned beef in all its forms replaced the exhausted stocks of fresh meat. In default of bread they nibbled sea biscuits. Langlais' humour did not improve on this regime.

In daylight one of the ships in the convoy drew close alongside the *Fidelity*. Barclay was on the bridge. At the sight of the Wren officer, the staff of the other ship grew wildly excited.

'We propose an exchange for an hour; two of our officers against that one of yours who is taking the air,' they signalled.

'OK' replied Langlais, 'we'll expect you.'

O'Neill was summoned in haste. His fine black beard made him look like a Viking.

'Here, put on this skirt and tunic and shove on this three-cornered hat.'

In this garb he leant against the rail at the exact spot which the girl had occupied a few moments before. The ships were side by side. Great shouts of enthusiasm came from the British ship. Pipite waited until the excitement was at its peak. Then he calmly turned round. Horrified, the English found themselves face to face with a bearded woman.

Langlais was delighted. He tapped the lieutenant affectionately on the shoulder and said:

'You look too sweet like that,' he said, 'I think you ought to marry Clébard.'

Contacts with his shipmates of the convoy were not always so gay. Langlais became more and more megalomaniac. On the pretext that one of the escorting sloops replied to his request for Gordon's Gin by offering to send another brand, he let them have a burst from his machine-gun.

This escapade was reported to the Admiralty and once more Johns had to use very considerable influence to arrange matters.

And the journey continued . . .

As they approached Gibraltar a landing craft weighing nearly three tons came loose from one of its moorings. It slid along the deck carrying away everything in its passage. After half an hour of fruitless effort, it had to be jettisoned. In the course of this manoeuvre one of the sailors was injured and had to be taken to the sick bay.

'If only the quack were here,' complained Lagrange.

He remembered the first trip during which the Belgian had cured his best friend of typhoid. Archibald remarked that this was the first time since O'Leary had disappeared that his name had been mentioned on board the *Fidelity*.

They did not put in at Gibralter. Their first mission consisted in picking up a group of North African French not far from Ténès. They stopped sixty miles off shore. After a few hours intensive work the *Fidelity* was transformed into a Brazilian cargo boat.

'It's a bastard to paint that flag,' said Richardson, who was always put on the stencils. 'Would you believe it – a globe, a coat of arms and a host of little stars.'

Langlais pulled his leg. 'You'll have to begin again, there's one missing. You'll get us spotted.'

In the wireless cabin, which was equipped with several transmitters, Langlais communicated on short waves to Johns. He announced that the operation had been confirmed. The following evening the ship approached the shore. A landing craft was lowered with Fontenay in command. The air was warm but unluckily there was a bright moon. They waited for a cloud to cover it so as to advance noiselessly with their oars. They could see the rugged contours of the Ténès coastal road and the rocky spur which served as an observation post.

'That's it,' said the lieutenant.

They sent the pre-arranged signals. No reply. They were repeated several times without success.

'We must go further in,' Fontenay said to the oarsmen.

Now they were a few yards from the bank. In the silent night when they listened carefully, they could hear the noises on land. A car passed high up on the hairpin bends, and they could hear the driver change gear half way up the hill. As soon as it had gone the officer signalled several times with his Aldis lamp. No reply.

'I'm sure we're on the right spot,' he swore.

He gave orders to start rowing again and when they were far enough out started the engine. They hugged the coast as far as Ténès. On a level with the harbour Fontenay gave the order: 'Put about.'

The plantation of pines was left behind and they returned to their starting point. Once more they rowed as far as the little creek.

No one in sight.

'We must return to the ship,' said the lieutenant. Dawn was about to break.

The hunchback was tidying up the paint room. Archie was cleaning the weapons; squatting tailor fashion and stroking his black beard, he was dismantling a Lewis gun which had jammed. Suddenly there was a burst of fire. The bullets ripped open the floor of the bridge, a few inches from Langlais' feet. Surprisingly cool-headed, the captain bent forward to his gunner.

'Archibald, the first principle to observe when you handle a loaded weapon in a ship is to point the gun out to sea,' and he added: 'With a bit of luck you'll hit a surfacing U-boat.'

He did not realize how prophetic his words were. That evening on their way to the Rhône delta where, on Johns' instructions, some agents were waiting to be picked up, a submarine surfaced to port, streaming with water. Friend or enemy? If they were to follow the wartime naval instructions, every unidentified submarine was an enemy. Archie rushed to his guns without bothering about the bogus passengers in their deck chairs. Langlais stopped him. 'Don't make a move, continue with your jobs as if you had a clear conscience. We're a Brazilian vessel.'

'Set your course for Marseilles,' he ordered the helmsman.

The U-boat commander must have had his doubts. He circled round the *Fidelity* which continued imperturbably on her way.

Archibald implored the captain, 'I promise I'll get him with the first burst.'

'No, the mission comes first.'

The nervous tension was unbearable. At any moment a track of foam could leave the U-boat in their direction. At this distance it would be fatal. At last, after an hour, the U-boat dived and was not seen again. But the incident had delayed the *Fidelity*. She arrived off Grau-du-Roi twenty-four hours after the appointed time. The mechanism of these appointments had to be as accurate as clockwork. Neither side was ever certain of meeting at the spot arranged. Those who waited ran great risks and sometimes had to let the friendly boat leave without showing themselves. In the case of the *Fidelity* her punctuality depended on the humour of the sea, the reliability of her engines and on unfortunate encounters.

Archibald was in command of the launch. He had no idea that the leader of the six men waiting for them was O'Leary who had escaped from his camp and had renewed contact through the Intelligence Service in Marseilles. The Belgian knew that it was the *Fidelity*. He saw the canoe approach the bank and send up its first recognition signals. He could not reply to them. The night before, on the date fixed, he had chartered a fishing boat to take him to the rendezvous. They had hoped in vain until five o'clock in the morning and on their return to the harbour the police had asked the fishing boat owner some awkward questions. Scared, the fisherman had refused to run the risk of a nocturnal sally a second time. Moreover, the alarm had been given and O'Leary and his five companions knew that they were under observation. They could not go down to the beach without giving themselves away and, at the same time, compromising those who had come to rescue them. Gnashing his teeth in his impatience, Mortiss watched the launch repeatedly fire its signals as it danced about the black waters like a firefly. For one moment he was afraid that it would land, but it put about and rowed off out to sea. A few moments later he heard the engine. Then there was silence. The liaison had failed.

Two days later they landed the second agent near Sète. He was an Englishman who had taken part in the Riff War and spoke excellent French. The men in the canoe left him on the

154

beach and Lagrange brought back two pockets full of sand from the expedition.

'French sand,' he kept saying to himself. 'At last I shall be able to convince my girl friend in Liverpool that they haven't got anything like it over there.'

Now they only had to land the last Gaullist agent. This was to take place between Oran and Algiers. Contrary to the custom aboard, the man had participated in the life of the ship. In – variably dressed in spotless white shorts and a Lacoste shirt, he had been nicknamed 'the tennis player'. At the start he thought of nothing but landings and adventures. However, Commander V's suicide, then the setbacks at Ténès and Grau-du-Roi and even more the approaching action, had progressively changed his ideas. When his turn came to land, he lost his nerve. In vain, the men in the launch tried to force him ashore. He merely shivered and had to be taken back on board.

When Langlais saw him he exploded with rage. The spectacle of fear disgusted him. He insulted the 'tennis player' in front of the whole crew, humiliated him cruelly and forced him to admit that he was scared.

'Admit that you have no guts!' he roared.

The man was almost green in the face.

'I'll take you to the beach myself,' said Langlais.

'No,' groaned the unfortunate man, 'I can't do it.'

'Coward!'

'No ... No ...'

The scene was ridiculous and abominable. It lasted too long. But Langlais could not control himself. He threatened to send the officer before a court martial. Finally he brought out his revolver.

'I give you the choice – either you land or you blow your brains out like your comrade did.'

It was ignoble. The agent collapsed physically. A familiar odour invaded the deck. Soiled and wretched, the man burst into tears like a child. He had to be taken down to his cabin.

The return to Gibraltar was sinister. The painting was carried out without enthusiasm and without a smile. The ship was at a loss. She crept into the harbour at night.

Brown was used to this. In his mind the *Fidelity* meant complications. He was not surprised, therefore, when he was woken up after curfew and told that Lieutenant-Commander Langlais wanted to speak to him at once.

'He must have had a scrap with someone,' Brown thought philosophically.

Langlais had come to tell him that of the three agents one had been landed according to plan, the second had committed suicide and the third was still on board, having refused to set foot ashore. As for the passengers they were supposed to pick up at Ténès and at Grau-du-Toi, there had been no sign of them. Their rashness had been ill rewarded; ill-luck seemed to dog the *Fidelity*. Brown, on the other hand, had a surprise for Langlais. Rogers had just arrived in Gibraltar, bringing excellent news of O'Leary and his companions.

On the top of the hill above Port-Vendres, the Belgian had thrown his blanket round the sailor's legs and run off into the vineyards. The guard hesitated for a moment and then rushed off in pursuit of him. Ford was now free. He carried on his way peacefully to Spain where he was interned. From there he reached Gibraltar, shortly after the *Fidelity* had left. Mortiss thought that he had outdistanced his adversary when, alarmed by the guard's cries, a peasant suddenly loomed up and barred his way. Before he had time to brush him aside, the sailor was on him. Flung to the ground and beaten, O'Leary was taken back to gaol where Rogers, Ferguson and the Monster soon joined him. Handcuffed, the four Gaullists were transferred to the Naval Prison at Toulon. O'Leary then conceived the idea of making his companions and himself pass for Canadian subjects.

The Monster, however, was obstinate and insisted that he was a French prisoner of war. Brought before an army examining magistrate, the three, one after the other, were asked to translate some lines from an original Shakespeare text. It was a disaster. O'Leary haughtily refused. 'Monsieur,' he said to the judge, 'if you had been to Quebec you would know that the inhabitants make it a point of honour not to understand English.'

Imprisoned at Fort Lamalgue and later at Saint-Hippolyte du Fort in the Gard, where British subjects were assembled, the three compatriots soon escaped. O'Leary directed operations. Rogers withdrew his parole at midday and left one minute later. Beneath the stupefied eyes of the guards the Belgian hoisted him on to his shoulders and let him jump over the wall. Landing on the other side, the chief engineer bumped violently into a young girl from the town whom he had been courting.

'Lend me your bicycle,' he said to her, taking it away by force. 'I'll marry you when I come back.'

He was not caught.

Then it was Ferguson's turn. O'Leary had bribed one of the camp officers. The phoney Canadian left in a French uniform with his papers in order and a warrant which allowed him a seventy-five per cent reduction on the railway.

O'Leary himself was the last to leave, after a long term of solitary and after seeing that the officer who had helped him escaped. Rogers knew no details, but he knew that it had caused a great stir.

'To sum up,' concluded the escaped man, 'if it goes on like this, no one will remain at Saint-Hippolyte except the two Englishmen who have given their word of honour not to try and escape and have not cancelled it . . .'

'But what are they waiting for? growled Langlais.

'They can't leave,' Rogers replied calmly. 'They are the ones who organize the escapes.'

They spent several days in Gibraltar. Archibald met the British pilot who boasted of having sunk the *Bismarck* with a single torpedo. When people looked incredulous the airman said: 'Yes, my bomb hit the rudder, the battleship could not manoeuvre. After that several ships pumped lead into her to send her to the bottom, but I was the one that really sunk her.'

Profiting by the calm water in the bay, Marcelac took the opportunity of getting in some training on his Petrel. The captain of the *Surcouf* had relinquished his only seaplane without too much fuss. The 'crate' could only take off in a dead calm sea and under the lee of a coast – in other words, in conditions when nobody would normally require it. Moreover, the *Surcouf* hangar was not sufficiently watertight in a dive and the Petrel was more of a nuisance than a weapon of combat. The same inconveniences applied in the *Fidelity* but Langlais looked upon his seaplane as a toy. On the least pretext he asked Marcelac to lower it on to the water and to make a tour round the bay. Fontenay was the first person to make the wisecrack: 'Marcelac has become the King's jester.'

As soon as their sailing date was known, they went to make their usual purchases in the Indian bazaar and had their last drinking outings ashore. They were memorably drunken evenings. The tolerant British naval police picked up the drunkards after curfew. Bundled into a truck, the unconscious sailors were dumped by their respective ships. If the cold night air woke them up they climbed aboard on their own. The officer of the watch was the judge of their capacity.

'Capable?' This meant that the man could stagger to his hammock.

'Incapable?' This meant that he would spend the night in the hold to get sober and to spare his mates the sight of his indignity. The inveterate drunkards who slept on the quayside were picked up and put on a charge sheet.

Once more they were bound for England. Langlais spent the time reviving the enthusiasm of his men. In the wardroom he maintained: 'The months of apprenticeship are over. A big mission awaits us in England.'

Doudet pretended not to hear and the rest of the officers were silent. Barclay sat like a sphinx but the captain supported his thesis with arguments.

'Dropping or picking up agents has never been an end but only the means. You can imagine that the British have not spent a fortune on this ship to send us cruising in the Mediterranean. Now we're off to war.'

They had heard too many of these phrases for them to carry any further weight. They hardly aroused a few mild curiosities, floating about like seaweed at the bottom of an aquarium. In actual fact everyone was discouraged. When they were off the coast of Spain three sailors, tired of Langlais' whims and harshness, jumped into the sea and swam ashore.

Harrow made the following entry in his diary: 'I am in a Dantesque ship with a crew of maniacs.'

A little later he added: 'It is a case of collective madness.'

CHAPTER TWELVE

WITH ALL HANDS

Waiting . . . eternally waiting. Even Archibald grew impatient. The *Fidelity* did not seem able to do anything but stand outside events. She kept approaching the goal without ever reaching it. One mission followed the other: they sailed, they painted, they camouflaged themselves. At night, with all navigating lights extinguished, a boat was lowered. It went into some creek to pick up escaped prisoners or to land mysterious passengers whose raincoats flapped in the sea wind.

As the months of exile increased these furtive nocturnal en-counters with their own lost country wrung their hearts. In the course of one of them, a sailor could not hold out any longer. As soon as he stepped ashore he fled into the dunes like a madman. They called him in vain. They had to re-embark the agents, arrange a new meeting place by radio, and land later further up the coast. The men of the *Fidelity* smelled the breath of war but never managed to get to grips with it. Wild beasts tethered out of reach of their bait, they began to growl.

On her return to Liverpool, the cargo vessel sweated despair. She looked like an old raddled woman with two much make-up on her face. With cracked paint and tar-strained, she stagnated at the quayside.

'She's no longer a ship – she's a hulk,' said Archie.

In spite of these disappointments, the *Le Rhône-Fidelity* retained her astonishing power of attraction on all those who had sailed in her. O'Leary, appointed by the Intelligence Service to ensure an escape line at Marseilles, had asked to rejoin his ship. A BBC message, 'Adolf must stay' had ordered the Belgian to remain at a post where he could render better service than in the *Fidelity*. Contrary to promises made to O'Leary, Langlais had not been consulted. When he learned several weeks later the step his second in command had taken, he flew into a rage.

'They steal my best officers from me!'

Rogers had already gone back to his engines, and the Monster returned in due course. Up before a naval court martial on the 20th September, 1941, he had got back to England thanks to O'Leary's organization. As though nothing had happened, as though the failed mission at Collioure had never taken place, he returned peacefully to his bunk, stuck his quid of tobacco to the hammock rope as usual and fell asleep. The following morning he merely said: 'You're a rum-looking lot.'

'What's odd about us?'

'Hm ... Hm ... you look as much like French sailors as a pair of sugar tongs looks like a spanner.'

By this time, the *Fidelity* had become a real British ship. The very air breathed in her was British. This slow transformation, accompanied by a leavening of British sailors, had caused some upsets among the crew. It was found one day that the paymaster responsible for the canteen and NAAFI provisions had stolen an important quantity of provisions and cigarettes. Langlais went down with him into the hold and hammered a sense of duty into him. They thought the matter would end there. But, irritated by the rumours current about the *Fidelity*, and presumably anxious to show his men that he treated the British culprit in the British manner – he sent him to the Admiralty. To strengthen his case he accused him of sodomy.

'This individual tried to seduce my seaplane pilot,' he maintained.

Marcelac suffered this final joke as he had suffered the rest. Was it not his role to amuse the captain?

At the end of the summer of 1942, Langlais himself was at the end of his tether. His behaviour betrayed a feverish impatience. He kept repeating to his fellow officers: 'We must strike a bold blow.'

Exasperated by this eternal waiting, his thirst for domination knew no bounds. Escorted by Mamadou or Daladier, carrying his gold-tipped cane, he quizzed his crew haughtily. Did the men complain? Where would they be without him? At the bottom of some Gaullist tub doing some tiresome coasting job. Did the officers complain? All of them owed their rank to him.

One evening in August Langlais sent for Archibald. For some weeks the relations between the two men had been strained. During a painting party the captain had reproached his gunnery officer of doing a bad job of camouflage on the funnel. Conscious of having done his work well, Archie had retorted:

'Well, if that's the case – I'm off!'

This was the first time the ex-airman had rebelled. He felt very bitter and Langlais tried to smooth things out.

'Well, Pilot,' he said, 'how's Nicole?'

Archibald's wife had presented him with a daughter in the spring.

'She's very well, sir, thank you.'

'Sit down.'

Bernard screwed up his eyes and puffed at his cigarette. This conversation embarrassed him. He thought it would bind him to something beyond his will.

'You know I always told you that the day you had a child I would release you,' said Langlais. 'Do you want to leave?'

'I'll see, sir.'

'If I ask you the question, it's because the time has come. Men who are prepared to die are rare. I have put in for and obtained a mission which will make the bravest man recoil.'

He had aged. The crowsfeet could be seen in the copper-coloured skin on his temples, his hair had turned white, and there was a great weariness in his features. But his eyes were still youthful.

'Before 1st January, I shall be either dead or a victor.'

His voice had remained the same – warm and convincing.

'The German U-boats refuel from a secret base near the Azores. That is the only explanation for the forays they make on our Atlantic convoys. They must be attacked in their lair.'

'With the *Fidelity*?'

'Yes.'

Langlais raised his eyes. 'Yes, with the *Fidelity*. If we wish to succeed, we mustn't go there in force. But we shan't be alone. The Monster will act as escort with a ship of small tonnage. Well, are you with me?'

Archibald shrugged his shoulders. 'Since you've decided . . .'

Langlais re-found his smile.

'I have a present for you. The British have sent me two seaplanes. You can have one of them.'

Terror could be seen on the airman's face.

'But, sir, I've never flown a seaplane and I haven't touched a joystick for two years.'

'You'll get by like a leader,' insisted Langlais.

A few days later two British airmen joined the *Fidelity*. The captain insisted that Archibald should have a training course on seaplanes.

'This is my pilot,' he said, introducing him to the instructor. 'He's an ace.'

For the uninitiated airman, taking off in a seaplane is no easy task, even in calm weather and in a sheltered bay. At his first attempt, Archie thought he was going to crash. The moment before he pushed forward his throttle he saw the blue sky in his windscreen and hardly felt a trace of seasickness. He pushed the throttle full home and suddenly – no more sky.

The sea seemed to have devoured it. The aircraft plunged

into the heart of a cascade. The pilot hastily set the windscreen wiper in motion. The crate sported on the waves like a porpoise, hesitated between being airborne and sinking into the water. Each time he touched the surface he ricocheted a little further in a spray of foam. Evenually he was airborne.

'Ugh!' said Archie.

The instructor understood. He gave this airman, who was less experienced than he had pretended, a course of dual control.

'Piti Lapin' had retired from business. A typed letter informed the officers and sailors of HMS *Fidelity* of the fact.

'She must have had it Roneod,' said Langlais.

The prostitute explained that, thanks to her generous monthly allowance, she had bought a typewriter and now intended to write her memoirs.

Langlais continued to lead a gay life. Alternately the Regent Palace and the Mayfair – where he booked two suites a year, one for himself and the other for his officers – closed their doors to him. For a time he stopped at the Piccadilly and then definitely adopted the Ritz. One evening he left the hotel to visit a night club. The air-raid warning went and within a few seconds a bomb fell on the establishment. The lights went out; there were cries and the sound of broken glass. Langlais was the first to notice that one of the dancing girls had fallen into the hole made by the bomb in the floor. Without a moment's hesitation he went down into the crater. When he came up at last covered with plaster, carrying the girl, the electric lights were on again. The guests crowded round him. By chance the girl was not injured. While they handed her a glass of brandy to revive her, she leaned with a blush towards her escort and whispered something in his ear. The latter gave a start and rushed at the captain of the *Fidelity*.

'Sir – you have done something disgraceful. Taking advantage of a woman's weakness, you have been lacking in respect.'

'Sir,' replied Langlais, 'I was unaware of it.'

When the man threatened him, he picked him up by the scruff of the neck and, paying no heed to the protests of the other customers, dropped him into the hole.

'Sir,' he said, 'you can judge for yourself if you can see what you're doing down there in the dark.'

The British autumn set in.

Archibald watched his captain's face for the gleam that would announce imminent action. Langlais was silent. Obstinate, blind and deaf, he renewed his visits to London and heaped recrimination on the authorities. But the 'little fellow' was playing for time. While considering the captain of the *Fidelity* an exceptional being, he deplored his exaggeration. The man was inhuman. He coveted neither money nor reward. The DSO which had once been one of his ambitions was today a joke. In these conditions he had to feed the beast and give him something to sharpen his teeth on.

With the organization of parachute drops in occupied country and the perfecting of the escape lines by land, the use of the *Fidelity* as a ship to transport agents diminished. The 'little fellow' could not possibly send him on further missions to the Mediterranean. Moreover, Langlais had refused them in advance.

'I'll never accept any more minor operations. In future I want real adventure. Do we leave for the Azores or not?'

Everything conspired against Langlais – world politics, the slowness of the Services, the conservatism of the Admiralty. Finally material details took a hand in the game. A sloop could not be found to suit the Monster. In default of anything better, the Breton equipped an American-built Newfoundland schooner which had been blocked in Northern Ireland by the war. She was not entirely suitable for the intended foray. Ploëno was given other tasks and he left the *Fidelity* on the 30th September. After a few days' hesitation the mission itself was cancelled.

Disillusion struck Langlais as lightning strikes a tree. When Archibald came and asked: 'Do you need me, sir?' the Corsican shook his head.

'The Azores is off,' he said. 'If you want to go, you're free.'

'I've put in for a transfer to the RAF.'

Langlais did not even seem grieved. By constantly frequenting British officers, he himself had acquired a kind of phlegm. He looked the lieutenant in the eyes: 'I shall miss you, Pilot.'

'I shall miss you, too, sir.'

O'Neill replaced Archie as gunnery officer.

'You guaranteed me death. Where is it?'

Banging his fist on the table, Langlais reproached Johns. The scars on his forehead and his jaw stood out like white furrows in his flushed face. He was obviously at the end of his tether.

'I won't leave here until you've given me a suicide mission. Don't you realize it's the only way you can get rid of me? Can't you understand that a Frenchman of my type has to demand death? There'll be a settling of accounts after victory. It will need many French corpses to restore the balance and to efface our shame. I and my men you can already write up in the profit column of France's balance sheet.'

There was a passionate plea in Langlais' request. Johns granted it. That evening when Langlais returned to Liverpool in his magnificent Daimler he looked like a man who has just got engaged.

At the beginning of November the *Fidelity* was sent to Portsmouth to be completely refitted once more. She was given twin gun turrets with 100mm automatics, four Oerlikons, four torpedo tubes, an asdic, an E-boat with two tubes, a radar apparatus, a large stock of depth charges and two Kingfishers for reconnaissance. This display of strength reassured the crew who had been afraid of finding themselves on an ack-ack ship defending some British port.

While the *Fidelity* was being rearmed for war, Langlais reorganized his staff. Mortiss' place was taken by Australian, Lt.-Cmdr. P. N. Bowman, Fontenay was promoted to Lt.-Cmdr., and O'Neill was given the auxiliary command of the landing craft.

The sleeping accommodation on the spar deck now housed 150 commandos. Their presence meant that departure was imminent. Langlais assembled his officers in the wardroom.

'Gentlemen,' he said, 'some of you may have thought that you were wrong to throw in your lot with me. Some of you have wondered if your fate was in the right hands. Today I can reassure these doubting Thomases. They no longer need worry about their future. They have none.'

He paused to see the effect of his words.

'I have no right to reveal to you the mission we are going to carry out, but I can promise you we shall not return. On this note, gentlemen, you have three days to go on the spree.'

Fontenay summed up the general impression.

'Although we know he always exaggerates, he's got something.'

Doudet was silent. In his view, this boded no good. Images of the ship being sunk with her flag flying and the second in command on the quarter deck must have flashed through his mind. He was not the leading figure and he had no wish to die. The war could very well have dispensed with him as a hero. In all probability, he had dreamed of a victorious return to Marseilles. It would be midsummer and La Joliette would be teeming with people in shirtsleeves. Reverting to her original name, the *Le Rhône* would draw alongside to the accompaniment of cheering.

'The *Le Rhône*, Captain Passementton,' the loudspeakers would blare, and the crowd would cry: '*Vive le Commandant!*'

The directors of the company would be at the foot of the gangway waiting to honour him.

Barclay looked upon the preparations with indifference. This noise of footsteps between decks, the foolish laughter of a crowd of men, the odour of bodies, sweating through the canvas of hammocks, obviously disgusted her. The commando boys were intruders. They had come on board to disturb her habits and her feminine possessive instinct was offended. She imagined the jokes they would be exchanging, coarse as the jokes of boys always are when they are in danger.

'One girl among a hundred and fifty. It won't give us long each.'

Why did she remain on board? If we can believe certain people, she could easily have got her discharge because she was tubercular. If this was true, why did she stay in the *Fidelity*? Some maintained that she was crazy about Langlais. Was she really his mistress? People eventually began to doubt it. No one could ever boast that they had seen her leave the Captain's quarters during the night. In eighteen months of communal life no one knew of any intrigue. Self-interest did not explain everything. Barclay knew that if she left for reasons of health, Langlais would continue to give her money. Nor can one say that she under-estimated the dangers she ran in the *Fidelity*. Her gilded cage was open and she had every reason in the world to fly away. She did not stir. Shut up in her cabin, she made a point of not altering the routine of her life on board. It seemed as though she did not wish to disturb anyone.

Notified of what was being prepared, Archibald arrived at Portsmouth. He was in RAF uniform and he shivered as he climbed aboard the old tub. Langlais was there supervising the preparations. The pilot shook his hand, and greeted Doudet, Fontenay, O'Neill and Rogers.

On deck everything had been changed once more. Archibald no longer recognized it. He tripped up over ropes, lowered his head clumsily before a landing-craft which had just been lashed. He no longer belonged to the *Fidelity*.

168

He visited Barclay in her cabin. She was smoking a cigarette in her bunk.

'Hullo, Archie!'

She seemed pleased to see him.

'So it's the big departure, it seems?' said the airman. She pointed to the place beside her on the bunk, near her head.

'Sit down.'

From his position, Archibald could look down at Barclay's face; her eyes stared at the ceiling.

'Yes,' said the girl wearily. 'It's the big departure.'

'Can one know where you're off to?'

She did not try to avoid the issue.

'To Indo-China. Langlais has persuaded the British to send a commando of 150 men there.'

'Naturally they'll be wiped out.'

She blew out a puff of smoke.

'Indo-China is a big place and he knows it well. He says there's a great deal of work to be done there. If they ever catch him he'll never get away.'

Archie sought for words, but they died on his lips.

'He'll succeed,' he said at last. 'He succeeds in everything he undertakes.'

Without getting up, Barclay stretched her ringed hand out to the lieutenant. 'Stub out my cigarette,' she said. Then she went on in the same expressionless voice: 'Langlais' a madman. He believes in his own words and he succumbs to his own charm. He's convinced that he'll always get away with it. He thinks that we shan't return from this mission, but he is certain of success. But *I know* that we shan't return . . .'

She put her hand in her trouser pocket, looking for her packet of Players. She fidgeted in the bunk and Archibald felt her head against his leg.

'Why are you going, then?' he asked.

She pursed her lips to light her cigarette and Archie gave her a light.

'I have always left with him,' she replied.

At dawn on the third day Langlais fell-in his commandos. Without giving them any explanation he put them in the train for London. When he reached the spot in the capital where he used to leave O'Leary in the old days, he ordered the OC detachment to get ready to march off.

It was a small street, indistinguishable from a hundred others. The rare passers-by wondered what such a concentration of troops could be doing in such a quiet district. At Langlais' command the soldiers marched off. He set out alone at the head of the column.

He marched as though the devil was at his heels. The commando officer did not see him slip into a doorway climb the stairs four by four and ring impatiently at an export-import office. A few minutes later the captain of the *Fidelity* was in Johns' office. He dragged the Englishman over to the window and parted the curtains slightly.

'Look at them,' he said to his bewildered companion. 'Take a good look at them. 'You'll never have a chance to do so again . . .'

The *Fidelity* disappeared with all hands.

APPENDICES

'The captain of U-435 reported the sinking of the *Fidelity* with three torpedoes between 16.00 and 17.00 hours on the 30th December, 1942.'

APPENDIX I

1.—Extract from *Marine et Résistance* by Admiral Muselier (page 25):

'On the 29th June, I left Gibraltar by air. On the morning of the 30th I was at the Admiralty in London. I had left at Gibraltar:

'(a) *Le Rhône*, commanded by Captain Passementton, reserve captain of corvettes, with Ensign Costa, charged with a special mission, and Ensign de Scitivaux of the Naval Air Service (Fighters), who had been seriously wounded in the arm.

'Only six men of *Le Rhône*'s crew had agreed to continue the struggle. In the course of a brawl caused by a discussion of rallying to Pétain, Ensign Costa was seriously wounded in the head; fifty officers and ratings were put ashore. The ship's complement was made up to strength once more with volunteers from the *Lieutenant-de-Vaisseau La Tour*, Belgian officers, French and Polish sailors, passengers evacuated from France on the *Anadyr* and the *Cap-Olmo*, others who had come over in the *President-Houduce* or from Spain . . .

'(e) Ensign Costa.'

2.—Report of the ship's boy P . . . put ashore at Gibraltar:

'On board, however, everyone was not of the same opinion. Most of the crew and the officers wanted to return to France. There was a brawl but I did not learn very much of the details. The sailors spoke in Corsican or kept silent in my presence.'

APPENDIX II
Specifications of the *Le Rhône*

Built in 1920 by M. & C. Grayson Ltd, 2,450 BRT; 5,000 m³; draught 20 feet; overall length 270 feet; 41 feet beam; MacKie & Baxter, Glasgow; triple-expansion engines; 1,100 h.p. two boilers; speed 9·5 knots; carrying capacity: 20 passengers in 7 cabins; 2 holds, 4 hatches; bought by the Company in 1923 from Messrs Devert & Chaumet for the transport of vegetable oils from Senegal.

The *Le Rhône* sailed on the Dakar-Saloum-Casamance run, then to the Black Sea ports and Morocco. Left the convoy on the 17th June, 1940, and put in at Gibraltar.

APPENDIX III
THE LAS PALMAS AFFAIR

1.—Report of the ship's boy P . . .:

'We said farewell to Las Palmas. Imagine my surprise in being woken up in the night with orders to fall in on the boat deck. To my stupefaction we made our way back to Las Palmas with all lights extinguished. We stopped. In the dark I could hear Captain Costa's orders to the sailors, telling them to be careful of the red objects they were carrying, for fear we blow ourselves sky high.

'This officer took his place in the launch, which was soon swallowed up in the darkness. Captain Passementton, at his post on the bridge, probably shared our anxiety. The coast and the twinkling lights of Las Palmas could clearly be seen and we wondered if we, for our part, were not visible from the shore. After a long wait, the launch flashed signals with an Aldis lamp and returned. We then left at full speed for Casablanca.'

1940

2.—SKL 10th May.

From Las Palmas comes a report that while in harbour the German steamer *Corrientes* was shelled with 15cm guns by a ship at sea. Investigations are in progress.

3.—*Weekly Naval Notes*, 16th May, 1940.

Canary Islands. The *Corrientes*, 4,565 tons, was damaged by an explosion aboard and rendered unseaworthy. She was towed into the inner harbour of Las Palmas by the *Ostmark* on the 10th May.

4.—Testimony of Ploëno, known as 'the Monster':

'Costa and Marais dived into the water near a German cargo vessel at anchor in the outer roads. These two officers succeeded in placing their charges against the hull of the *Corrientes* and returned safe and sound on board the *Le Rhône*. The operation was facilitated by the presence of coal lighters round the cargo vessel which made observation difficult. The charges exploded with the desired results.'

APPENDIX IV

1.—Testimonies are conflicting as to the loss of the *Fidelity*.

Peter O'Neill – in command of the launch which was lowered during the attack – is categorical. He dates the action off the Azores between Christmas Eve and Christmas Day 1942. These waters were infested with submarines. The ship in which the commodore of the convoy was flying his flag had been sunk. The *Fidelity*'s aircraft had crashed into the hull, causing damage to the condenser. The second plane was airborne. The launch spotted several U-boats and had attacked the nearest with depth charges. An engine breakdown forced her to break off visual contact. Nevertheless, she remained in radio communication with *Fidelity* all night. In the morning there was total silence.

O'Neill and his shipmates jettisoned her damaged turret, made a jury sail of blankets and set course for England, twelve hundred miles away. After a week's sailing by dead reckoning, they met a British warship which took them in tow. The hawser broke twice and the launch had to be sunk after her crew had been taken off.

2.—HMS *Fidelity* (Loss of):

(1) In December 1942, after a special refit, HMS *Fidelity* sailed to join the Eastern Fleet. She carried two aircraft, a launch and a few small landing craft.

(2) She joined a convoy bound for Freetown under the command of Vice-Admiral W. D. M. Egerton, DSC (Ret.).

(3) In the neighbourhood of the Azores the convoy was subjected to a very heavy attack by German U-boats. The action began early in the morning of 27th December. Several ships were sunk that day, and those that got away could not pick up

all the survivors. HMS *Fidelity* was detailed that evening as rescue ship.

(4) The enemy attack continued throughout the 28th December. During the afternoon the escort Captain D. asked *Fidelity*, in spite of the high sea running, to dispatch one of her aircraft in defence of the convoy. The attempt was abortive and the aircraft crashed into the sea. Its crew was picked up by one of the escorting destroyers.

(5) On the evening of the 28th more ships were sent to the bottom, including the commodore's flagship. HMS *Fidelity* was delayed; her engines had suffered damage when the aircraft crashed into her hull. An escort ship remained with her until the morning of 29th December. This ship then received orders to rejoin the convoy and Gibraltar was requested to send a tub to help the *Fidelity*. The ship advanced slowly. In the morning she sighted another destroyer and by the afternoon had managed to repair the engines sufficiently to continue on her way. She sent a message that she was making for the Azores. The second aircraft, which had taken off to carry out a reconnaissance, was hoisted aboard on its return.

Later the *Fidelity* sent a signal that she had spotted two U-boats and was going in to engage them. The launch had already been lowered to participate in the action. Shortly after this a U-boat was again sighted and the launch and the small boats, which had been lowered for this purpose, tried to attack it – but without result.

(6) Shortly after 20.00 hours HMS *Fidelity* picked up the commodore of the convoy, Vice-Admiral Egerton, and a few members of his crew.

(7) Shortly after midnight the engine of the launch began to fail and contact was broken with *Fidelity*. Radio contact continued until about 21.00 hours on the 30th December. The launch was picked up by a destroyer.

(8) Nothing more is known of the fate of the *Fidelity*. On the 30th December a destroyer escort was dispatched and

continued the search until 7th January. They found no trace of *Fidelity*. The Admiralty deduced that she must have been lost during the night of the 31st December, 1942/1st January, 1943. In consequence, the 1st January, 1943, is the presumed date of her loss.

(9) The above information is based on details given by the crew of the launch and the first aircraft, combined with the radio signals sent from the *Fidelity*.

(10) Other information concerning this loss has since been obtained from prisoners, who declared that a vessel – its description corresponds exactly to the *Fidelity* – was attacked by their U-boat towards the end of December, seen again on the following day, and sank on the third day. This proves that the date of the loss was the 31st December, 1942.

(11) The fact that the crews of the aircraft and the launch were picked up separately gave rise to rumours that there were other survivors of the *Fidelity*. Not a single survivor was picked up by the British warships. Nevertheless, the Admiralty was unable to confirm the rumours that a few prisoners had been taken by the U-boats.

3.—Historical Archives of the Royal Navy.

December 1942. HMS *Fidelity* was ordered to join the Eastern Fleet. Joined the Freetown convoy ONS 154 which was subjected to serious U-boat attacks off the Azores. Engine breakdown. Launch lowered to pick up surivors. Broke down in turn with the result that the *Fidelity* and the launch were left behind by the convoy. The launch lost sight of *Fidelity* in the early morning of 30th December and was later picked up by a destroyer. A destroyer flotilla, having searched without success for the *Fidelity* or her survivors, the Admiralty declared her 'presumed lost on the night of the 31st December, 1942/1st January, 1943.'

4.—Testimony of Ploëno, known as 'the Monster':

During January 1943 Radio Hamburg broadcast that a certain German submarine had sunk a small British auxiliary cruiser, heavily laden, sailing at reduced speed, on a certain course, at such and such degrees of longitude and latitude, which corresponded perfectly to the movements of the *Le Rhône-Fidelity*.

5.—HMS *Fidelity* Casualty List:

OFFICERS

Missing Presumed Killed:

*Temporary Commander J. Langlais, RN (In command).

Temporary Lieutenant (A) J. J. Avencourt, RNVR.

First Officer M. Barclay, WRNS.

Temporary Acting Lieutenant-Commander P. N. Bowman, DSC, RNVR.

Temporary Lieutenant A. Bull, RNVR.

*Temporary Lieutenant-Commander R. W. Doudet, RN.

*Temporary Acting Lieutenant-Commander P. R. Fontenay, RN.

*Temporary Lieutenant R. J. Lalande, RN.

Temporary Acting Sub-Lieutenant J. P. T. Martin, RNVR.

Lieutenant-Commander J. W. F. Milner-Gibson, DSC, RN.

*Temporary Lieutenant (E) H. Patterson, RN.

Temporary Paymaster Lieutenant R. L. Paul, RNVR.

Surgeon Lieutenant J. Robertson, RN.

*Temporary Sub-Lieutenant (E) R. Starness, RN.

*Temporary Lieutenant C. Stone, RNVR.

Temporary Paymaster Lieutenant C. F. Thunder, RNVR.

Lieutenant-Commander (E) W. B. White, RNR.

* Indicates Free French personnel serving in the Royal Navy.

Missing Presumed Killed:

Brown, Edward M.	Steward	P/LX 24977
Cambon, Charles L.	Acting Petty Officer	FAA/FX 115190
Christophe, Jean R.	Acting Chief Motor Mechanic	P/MX 99523
Dunne, Bernard	Engine Room Artificer 4th Class	P/MX 69518
Gilson, George	Leading Writer	P/MX 72199
Glenton, Ralph	Shipwright 4th class	P/MX 72164
Jock, Charley	Leading Seaman	P/JX 251826
Lagrange, Robert L.	Ordnance Artificer 4th Class	P/JX 221680
Langevin, Georges C.	Leading Seaman	P/JX 221679
Leaver, William	Leading Stoker	P/KK 116961
Le Franc, Jean L.	Leading Seaman	P/JX 221678
Marsh, Marcel	Acting Leading Seaman	P/JX 214400
Norton, Charles F.	Leading Seaman	P/JX 251752
Patrick, Eugene E.	Leading Seaman	P/JX 221677
Pearson, Henry J.	Leading Seaman	P/JX 214416
Powell, Roger	Telegraphist	P/JX 225850
Robbs, Guy	Able Seaman	P/JX 224894
Sharrock, Roger	Acting Leading Stoker (Ty.)	P/KX 116237
Stokes, John	Able Seaman	P/JX 207904
Thorne, Robert	Able Seaman	P/JX 214398

6.—Citation by order of the French Republic of the officers and men of *Le Rhône*.

Decision No. 144 of the 11th April, 1946, GPRF, signed F. Gouin (*Journal Officiel* of the 21st May, 1946, special pagination 1334 G).

'The Q-ship *Le Rhône* which joined the Free French forces in June 1940 and was incorporated into the Royal Navy under the name of HMS *Fidelity*, with French officers and crew under the command of Capitaine de Corvette Costa, carried out important special missions. She disappeared gloriously with all hands off the Azores in December 1942, while escorting a convoy under attack from German U-boats.

'This citation includes the award of the Croix de Guerre with Palm to Capitaine de Corvette Costa.

'This decision will be published in the *Journal Officiel* of the French Republic.'

Although the appendices are from official texts we have preserved the transformed French names as they figure on page 7.

APPENDIX V

Service Record in the Royal Navy of Claude Andre Michel Costa (Alias Jack Langlais)

Date of joining the Royal Navy: 1st July, 1940.

Rank: Acting Lieutenant-Commander RN, 1st July, 1942 (back-dated to 16th March, 1940).

Appointment: Posted to command HMS *Fidelity*, 6th September, 1940.

Reported missing: 30th January, 1943.

Probable date of death: 1st January, 1943.

Appreciations:

1. Lieutenant-Commander Langlais was oppointed OC HMS *Fidelity* shortly after his arrival in the United Kingdom. Until the end of 1941 he carried out two operations in the Mediterranean and a series of complicated landings of agents, singly or in small groups.

2. This officer displayed all the qualities of a leader – courage, energy, zeal, and a loyalty and enthusiasm which can only be termed as outstanding. He was an eminently competent naval officer. His methods of maintaining discipline on board his ship were unorthodox, even if one takes into account that the methods in the Royal Navy were unfamiliar to him, but he maintained discipline and obtained results.

3. He met with almost insurmountable difficulties in the rearmament of his ship and in the obtaining of the equipment he considered necessary. He never took 'no' for an answer, and always got his own way in the end.

4. When HMS *Fidelity* was considered unsuitable for landing operations, Lieutenant-Commander Langlais approached Sir James Somerville, the ex-C.-in-C. Mediterranean. Thanks to his help and encouragement the *Fidelity* was re-armed for raids and commando operations in South-Eastern Asia, where Sir James had been appointed Naval C-in-C. The *Fidelity* was lost with nearly all her crew on her way to the Far East.

5. The main characteristic of this remarkable personality, among various other eminent qualities, was his loyalty to France, to Great Britain and to his superiors in the Royal Navy.

(Assistant Secretary to the Admiral)

APPENDIX VI

REPORT OF COMMANDER B—, RN

I met Lieutenant-de-Vaisseau Costa for the first time just after the collapse of France, when he brought his ship into Gibraltar. Not all the members of his crew had come voluntarily; they had been 'persuaded' to act in this way by Costa on the high seas. The *Le Rhône* was laden with provisions and war material of all kinds, which Costa immediately placed at the disposal of the Gibraltar authorities.

When orders came from the French C-in-C Mediterranean that the ship and her crew were to make for Moroccan territory, the French liaison officer ordered Costa to accompany him. The latter refused to do this and asked me whether he could serve Great Britain. This request was granted and he remained with his ship in Gibraltar until arrangements could be made. Shortly after this Costa received a second order from the French admiral to return to Morocco. Once more he refused, and in consequence was informed that he had been condemned to death for treason, for not having carried out the orders received.

About this period various refugees from Gibraltar returned there from Casablanca. They arrived in boats which were indescribably filthy and they had sailed under the worst possible conditions. Costa immediately sent to these vessels an apology for the treatment inflicted by the French authorities in Morocco and supplied them with a considerable quantity of provisions.

The *Le Rhône* left Gibraltar at the beginning of 1940 flying the Blue Ensign. During its stay in Great Britain the ship was camouflaged as a British cargo vessel and put into commission as HMS *Fidelity*. Costa assumed the name of Langlais and was given the rank of lieutenant-commander in the Royal Navy. He signed on a crew of Frenchmen who were serving in the Royal Navy. Lieutenant-Commander Milner Gibson, DSC, was appointed as his liaison officer.

In 1941, HMS *Fidelity* carried out two special missions in the Mediterranean, returning to Great Britain after each of them for repairs and refits. The second journey showed that she was no longer suitable to be employed further in this capacity in the Mediterranean, but Lieutenant-Commander Langlais did not wish to leave his ship. He put forward vast plans for *Fidelity* to be used in Far-Eastern waters of which he had acquired considerable experience in the past. These plans were accepted and the vessel underwent a new transformation in Great Britain.

When the *Fidelity* was ready, Lieutenant-Commander Langlais took her to Scotland for a long, intensive training. In recognition of his services to the Navy he was promoted to Commander – the only French officer to receive this distinction. At the end of 1942 his ship was ready to sail for the Far East and was sunk in convoy in circumstances which have already been described. With Commander Langlais we lost Lieutenant-Commander Milner Gibson, DSC, and the British commandos.

I have sent with this report a copper plaque presented to Langlais (then Costa) by his fellow-officers (of the *Le Rhône*) on the completion of a certain successful mission. Langlais gave me this plaque the last time I saw him.

If after the War his family wishes to hear verbally other details of Langlais's life they can always communicate with me at the Admiralty.

APPENDIX VII

From a report, tape-recorded on 23rd January, 1957, by Capt. FRANCOIS MARCEL BASIN, Officier de la Légion d'Honneur, MBE, a British Secret Service agent under Col. Buckmaster, and a pioneer of the French Resistance Movement.

Capt. Basin, Lt. Bruce Cadogan and Lt. Dollan were the three agents taken on board the *Fidelity*. Receiving them in his cabin, Langlais pointed to a portrait of King George VI and said, 'That's my boss. You are now in one of His Majesty's ships.'

Basin observed the ship's collapsible panels, the lifeboats cut in two to conceal machine-gun nests, crates of 'fruit' which were depth-charges, and the hangar which housed the seaplane. The ship maintained a 'tail-end Charlie' position behind the convoy, to act as a decoy for U-boats and aircraft, though, as Basin was told, 'If a tin-fish hits us with what we've got in our holds, we'll be blown to Kingdom Come.'

Basin remembered well the suicide of Commander V (see page 149, as he was ordered by Langlais to make an inventory of the dead man's belongings. 'It's a bloody disgrace!' shouted the Corsican. 'In wartime an officer has no right to commit suicide.'

The convoy consisted of thirty-four ships when it left Greenock; a few days out from Gibraltar only eleven remained. During the voyage the *Fidelity* changed her identity twice, once with the sailors dressed as women passengers dancing on deck while an enemy aircraft flew overhead.

Off the Balearic Islands one evening a surfaced U-boat challenged the *Fidelity* to identify herself. Although receiving no reply, her commander appeared to assume that the *Fidelity* was a submarine supply ship and made no attempt to stop her.

Two nights later, Langlais called Basin to his cabin and gave him his landing instructions. With a compass, a Colt revolver, and a small bag of clothes, Basin was rowed to the coast; stark naked, he waded ashore.

A message which he had sent back to his family via another agent said: 'The crew of the *Fidelity* look upon me as a hero because I'm going to land in France and take the risk of falling into the hands of the Boche. They're wrong. I'm in a hurry to leave. The real heroes are those who remain in such a ship.'